D1217602

THE CONTRIBUTORS

JACOB NEEDLEMAN, professor of philosophy at San Francisco State University, is author of *The New Religions* and *A Sense of the Cosmos.*

FATHER WILLIAM JOHNSTON, S.J., has lived in Japan for more than twenty years and is the author of *The Still Point, Christian Zen,* and *Silent Music: The Science of Mysticism.*

LOBSANG P. LHALUNGPA was born in Lhasa, Tibet, and is presently director of a Tibetan-studies institute in Vancouver. He is also engaged in translating the sacred texts of Tibetan Buddhism.

LIZELLE REYMOND is the author of *My Life with a Brahmin Family, To Live Within,* and, most recently, *Shakti.*

SEYYED HOSSEIN NASR is the author of *The Encounter of Man and Nature, Ideals and Realities of Islam,* and *Sufi Essays.*

DOM AELRED GRAHAM is a Benedictine monk of Ampleforth Abbey, England. Among his numerous books are *Zen Catholicism, Conversations Christian and Buddhist,* and *The End of Religion.*

P. L. TRAVERS, although best known as the author of the world-famous *Mary Poppins,* has been a lifelong student of mythology and fairy tales as bearers of psychological and metaphysical teachings.

PHILIPPE LAVASTINE is a well-known French scholar who has lived and traveled extensively throughout Asia.

Sacred Tradition and Present Need

An Esalen Book

BY JACOB NEEDLEMAN

A Sense of the Cosmos

The New Religions

The Sword of Gnosis (Editor)

Being-in-the-World

Religion for a New Generation
(Editor, with A. K. Bierman and James A. Gould)

Sacred
Tradition
and
Present
Need

Edited by Jacob Needleman and Dennis Lewis

The Viking Press   New York

LIBRARY OF CONGRESS CATALOGING IN PUBLICATION DATA
Main entry under title:
Sacred tradition and present need.
(An Esalen book)
First presented as a series of lectures sponsored by
Esalen Institute in San Francisco during the summer of 1973.
1. Spiritual life—Addresses, essays, lectures.
I. Needleman, Jacob. II. Lewis, Dennis.
III. Esalen Institute.
BL624.S2   248'.4   75-14498
ISBN 0-670-61441-6

Printed in U.S.A.

Preface

The current spiritual ferment in California epitomizes the yearning of twentieth-century man for catalytic answers to the fundamental questions of existence. The new religions; experiments with meditation and other religious techniques; attempts at self-exploration and human relations through sensory awareness, encounter, and communes have now spread throughout the world.

The series of lectures "Sacred Tradition and Present Need," presented in San Francisco during the summer of 1973, was an attempt to turn away from all this ferment. Our question was: Has the "spiritual revolution" lost its direction in a profusion of innovations? In our haste to reject outworn religious forms, customs, and ideals, have we overlooked the truths that have guided traditional life and thought since time immemorial? And can the ancient traditions cut through our present confusion and speak anew to Western man's need?

I was very glad when Esalen agreed to sponsor this series of lectures. For in the present ferment, Esalen has played a decisive role and has become known as a center and point of origin in the innovative approach to personal growth. What better context could there be in which to face directly the crisis in modern man's relationship to the sacred?

Most important was the selection of speakers. They had to be authoritative representatives of traditional spirituality, in contact with the practical, "mystical" heart of the ancient teachings, yet also willing to communicate with so many of us who have spent our lives outside these realms of the traditional.

In some cases, no one came forward to undertake this task. For example, the representatives of Zen Buddhism very interestingly explained their reluctance to present their teachings in a public setting. Their way is open, they said, to any who seek them, but they did not wish to *initiate* the exchange. And in a remarkable conversation, Krishnamurti also declined our invitation for reasons that cut deep into the whole question of the limits of traditional forms in the present age. He told the story of a deeply religious man who revered a statue of the Buddha, "a wonderful wooden statue. One winter the man became very cold and had nothing left to burn in his fire. The Buddha appeared to him in the middle of the night and said, 'Burn me.' "

We thus fell far short of our aim in representing the entire spectrum of spiritual traditions, including those which do not refer to themselves as traditional. But imperfect as our efforts of organization were, we have chosen to collect them in this book, together with excerpts from the period after each lecture when the speakers opened themselves to searching questions from the audience. Each talk in its own right is a perhaps never-to-be-repeated gesture from a world most of us have until now been unable to appreciate, despite our storming at the gates of the spiritual search.

JACOB NEEDLEMAN

Acknowledgments

I wish to express my gratitude to Michael Murphy, who, as president of Esalen Institute, appreciated the need for this series of lectures and supported it at every turn. I am also grateful to Bishop Kilmer C. Myers of the Episcopal Diocese of California and especially to Mrs. Elizabeth Bussing for their efforts in making available Grace Cathedral, which was the setting for these talks.

I wish also to thank the Marsden Foundation of New York and the Far West Institute of San Francisco for the help that enabled me to invite exactly those speakers who could make this series a study in the communication of universal ideas.

J. N.

Contents

Sacred Tradition and Present Need

The Used Religions

Jacob Needleman

. . .

.

MODERN MAN, disenchanted by science and by the established forms of his religion, suddenly finds arrayed before him religious teachings emanating out of worlds and times he has never known. From the Orient and the Near East, ancient systems that in the past have been for us little more than food for fantasy now seem to offer themselves as live options, each promising us a renewed and sacred relationship to our own being and to the cosmos that contains us.

One may even detect the apparent stirrings of the ancient contemplative traditions of Christianity and Judaism. Ideas that were once burned into man through the fires of spiritual discipline and an all-encompassing moral code are now, it seems, published and explained by almost everyone, almost everywhere. Not only ideas, however, but spiritual forms and psychophysical disciplines are being brought here by teachers and holy men representing a broad spectrum of alien cultures. Around these teachers from the East gather thousands of people, young and old, drawn by the power of experiences such as were never vouchsafed to them by church or synagogue or by the secular religion of psychiatry.

For anyone who has not been blind and deaf during the past twenty years this development is astounding. One might have expected that political upheavals and advanced technology would produce a superficially internationalized world in the area of economics or in the arts, or on the external levels of religious fashions. But knowing that the great religious founders of the past deeply embedded their teachings in the milieu of a specific culture with all its special needs and psychic traits, and recognizing that the passage of a genuine teaching from one culture to another is an event nearly as extraordinary and rare as the original appearance of the teaching itself, one may well be skeptical. Two of the great missionary teachings of the world, Christianity and Buddhism, transformed the life of entire peoples—but over long periods of time and, particularly in Buddhism, working quietly and from within. In Tibet and China, for

1

example, centuries passed before the impulse given by Padmasambhava or Bodhidharma was reflected in the general culture. And who knows what took place between the time when the first Christians migrated to Britain and the time when the forms of Celtic Christianity touched the existence of all men living there? How many hundreds of years passed while the deserts of the Near East sheltered the early cenobites? Is so much time and silence needed for the gathering of a certain energy?

I am writing as a Californian, a man without tradition who hears all around him claims of a "spiritual revolution" being made not only by the representatives of alien traditions but by countless people like himself who have hardly ever felt the breath of traditional spirituality in their lives. Without much real concern for the historical background, many of these thousands see the present moment as the beginning of a new age.

They are confident the future will be different from the past.

But other voices tell us that, far from being a sign of an awakening, this phenomenon of the "new religions" is only the most recent turn in modern man's descent into total materialism: the movement from antitraditionalism to an even more sinister "countertraditionalism" in which the truth of ancient teachings is "parodied" through the same forces of exploitation that have defined the entire modern era.

What will help us find our way out of this ambiguity? I ask the question as a Californian. Is it true that the ancient spiritual teachings are now coming forward and offering themselves as living alternatives to Western man? Is it in America, in California—where scarcely a trace remains of traditional civilization—that this astonishing transaction will be made? Or is it too late for everything except imitation, enthusiastic commitment, and the other devices by which confusion is masked?

Out of these questions yet another question arises, perhaps even more fundamental: *Are the forms by which truth was once transmitted inapplicable to the present conditions of human life?* Can we discover with precision the specific point of failure in the relationship between ourselves and the sacred? For, *without knowing how to find this point of failure, how will we situate ourselves at the correct point of effort?* And if we cannot so situate ourselves, will not everything that is presented to us as spiritual struggle be largely a waste of time, or even worse?

Our question is twofold: who has failed—ourselves or the traditions? What is the real hiddenness and the real corruption of tradition?

It was with such questions in mind that I recently traveled through Europe, and I offer the following recollection in the hope of opening these issues further. For what it meant to be an American, a modern man, a Californian, finally began to be clear to me at the end of my tour, among the monasteries of Mount Athos.

I had often dreamed of visiting this place, the monastic heart of the Eastern Church. Cut off from the world for a thousand years, was it a Western Tibet where there still existed the knowledge and methods of esoteric Christianity? I mean the knowledge of man's true weaknesses and hidden possibilities, as well as the techniques of inner prayer, bodily discipline, and communal relationship that could destroy the weaknesses and bring forth the possibilities. I was convinced that such knowledge was not the special preserve of the Oriental traditions. Yet I had never found anything in the existing forms of Western Christianity to support my conviction. My purpose was to discover if these ancient spiritual practices of Western Christianity were coming to life again. Yet my search had so far turned up only one tantalizing hint outside the shadows of the Vatican— a word spoken by a magnetic woman, a devout Christian mystic, who said only that the Church had kept its secrets too well. What secrets? She did not wish to say more.

And so it was with intense anticipation that I was carried along the rugged Aegean coast toward the peninsula of Athos on the last leg of my journey. I tried to maintain a realistic sense of restraint, for I had been warned from all sides that the cenobitic tradition was dying here and that many of the monasteries were now abandoned relics tended only by a few die-hard monks. The population, I was told, had sunk from twenty thousand monks to a low of fifteen hundred and was still declining.

I will not go into great detail about the appearance of the island and its ancient monasteries, the dense vegetation, the stench of compost filling the air, the disarray and windy desolation of the official buldings, and, for me, the pervasive impression of something disturbingly familiar: the bearded, patriarchal monks in their black robes going mechanically about their business in ways that resembled the orthodox Jews I knew in my childhood. I traced this sense of familiarity to the feeling I always had as a child when forced to participate in the austere forms of a tradition that was meaningless to me and that had no right in my world.

From the very first step on Athos the questions rang in my mind: what *is* tradition? Is there a life I cannot see within these forms? Is it because I lack real spiritual hunger? But if that is so, what do I—what do we—hunger for when we ask over and over again about the meaning of our existence and when we feel the contradictions— which no science or philosophy has resolved—between the narrowness of our lives and the vast universal forces of death, creation, and cosmic harmony? If a spiritual tradition cannot meet us on the ground of this hunger for meaning, then with whom does the failure lie?

Before taking to the trails, I sat for a while in the Cathedral of Karyes, the central village of the peninsula. In the Gothic cathedrals of Western Europe one is instantly shocked into silence by their immeasurable vertical spaces, until gradually the extraordinary light breaking in through the stained-glass windows gently lifts one upward. The universe of the Gothic cathedral is to me immense and merciful. But the Orthodox church is dark as a starry night, lit mainly by scattered flickering candles. In this space one is everywhere closely surrounded by the powerful icons, radiating as though by their own light. One's eyes move over walls covered with stars against a night-blue background, stopping suddenly at the great dome above, upon which a gigantic head of Christ looks back down at you. This is a cosmos whose central force is an act of sacrifice for the sake of man, for oneself. And this sacrificial cosmos demands from man a response. But by the time I left Athos I was wondering from where in us this response could possibly come.

After several hours of hiking I came to the fortress-like Stavroniketa monastery jutting out dramatically over the sea on the eastern coast of the peninsula. By custom, each monastery is obliged to take in all sojourners and provide them with food and lodging. But I was turned away at Stavroniketa: because of repairs there was no room for guests.

No amount of persuasion on my part (in an exchange of clumsy gestures and broken English) had any effect. I was tremendously disappointed, having heard that at this monastery something might be found. And of course I knew that, had they really wished, they could surely have taken in a single guest for the night. It was late in the afternoon and, since the monasteries close their doors at sundown, I wearily stood outside the Stavroniketa pondering my next move. Huge storm clouds were gathering overhead, leaving me with the prospect of a dash of several kilometers down the coast.

What was I looking for? I realized, standing there, that I was traveling blind. Did I expect to encounter some aged hermit with piercing eyes who would take me in and reveal to me the secrets of his practice? Or would the abbot of some great monastery allow me to participate in the rituals of his inner circle? Moreover, I spoke no Greek, so that in addition to everything else I was naïvely hoping for a miracle of language as well.

How far I was from California! Not once during all my earlier investigations of the new religious groups of America did I ever feel something was being held back from me. Whether it was a Zen monastery or a Sufi group or a fledgling ashram, always the leaders invited me in. Even when told it was an esoteric teaching, I had little difficulty arranging to participate as much as I wished; and even when warned that there were things that could not be spoken about to outsiders, I found that sooner or later more information was given to me than I had asked for. All that had surprised me at first, but I soon came to take it for granted. Now, however, and in the next twenty-four hours, I was again faced with the question as to the nature of spiritual reserve and the maturity of California religion.

I was about to give up and move on when, as though out of nowhere, there appeared a layman who addressed me in perfect English. I told him what I was and what I was looking for, and, to make the story brief, in two hours I found myself high in the turret of the monastery in a spacious, austere guest room. Seated across from me was Father Vassilios, abbot of Stavroniketa. This was the setting of the long conversation that then took place between Father Vassilios and me. I believe that in this conversation it may be possible to find the essential questions we in the modern world need to place before all of the traditional teachings that are offering themselves to us.

The sky had cleared, and through the wide-open windows the room was lit by the twilight and the rising moon reflected off the sea. We sat around a heavy plank table—Father Vassilios in his black robes and hat, and our interpreter, a young professor of medicine from Athens who wished to be known only by the name Evangelos.

As for Father Vassilios, he did not seem very much older than I—in his mid-forties, perhaps, slender and athletic with aquiline fea-

tures, a full, black beard, and noncommittal, steady eyes. I began
by describing to him the profusion of new religious groups in America, the influx of teachers from the East, and the massive movement
away from established religious forms by the young. I chose to emphasize the fact that most of these new religions bring with them
practical methods such as meditation, chanting, Yoga exercises, and
the like which seem to provide real experiences of something Christianity and Judaism have only been talking about. I had in the back
of my mind an interesting comment made to me only a week before by an official at the Vatican. He had said that for too long
there had been a fear of spiritual experiences—as though people had
ceased to believe that God is good enough to give such experiences.

"It is not a question of methods," said Father Vassilios. "It is a
question of the whole of life. These methods produce hallucinations.
What do I mean by hallucinations? People search after experiences,
not truth. One must begin by accepting truth and feeling truth.
Only then can 'method' enter in the right way."

I found this reply very interesting. There was something *contemporary* in it, which I suppose I should have anticipated from a few
facts I had gleaned from Evangelos about the abbot's background.
He had studied for several years in Paris (our conversation took place
in a mixture of French, Greek, and English) and he was, I gathered,
the only abbot on Athos who had been involved even to that extent
in modern Western culture.

"But," I said, "our religions in the West long ago reached the
point where they seemed incapable of providing new experiences.
The young—and the older generation—finally have reacted to this
lack. Is it so wrong to look for special experiences? When life loses
its meaning—then what else should a man struggle for if not for a
new contact with reality? a new quality of experience?"

After a slight pause, he answered with one word, "Faith."

He waited while I tried to digest that. I felt a wave of disappointment. Yes, I understood his answer; it was good Christian doctrine;
in a way it was the great truth. But in another way, the great truth
was not enough and could not be enough for us. We needed more
than pure truth; we needed help. For twentieth-century man, was
there enough psychological help in the answer 'faith'?

From Father Vassilios I felt an immediate awareness of my disappointment. I have interviewed many religious leaders before and
since meeting Father Vassilios. With very many of them—the representatives of the "new religions" no less than church officials—I have

felt that their replies to my questions were preformulated. But it seemed to me that some were searching for their own truth at the very moment of their replying to me, reconstituting their understanding, as it were, out of the unknown. The ring of authority, which is a much more mysterious factor than we imagine, existed for me only in the latter cases. Father Vassilios seemed constantly to be shifting between these two "places."

Of course, the quality of my questioning was probably not such as to deserve more than doctrinaire answers. I think we must bear that factor in mind when we try to put questions to the great traditions. We so easily assume that our questions deserve great answers.

"One must *begin* with faith," he said, "and from that God adds what is necessary. Anything else is human invention."

"In America," I said, "many young people begin with the prayer of Jesus."

I expected him to raise his eyebrows at this because I knew that in the Orthodox tradition it is considered dangerous to practice the prayer of Jesus, the repetition of the phrase "Lord Jesus Christ have mercy on me," without the guidance of a spiritual director. I felt I was still not getting across to him what psychological method means to us in America. In fact, throughout my travels in Europe I was amazed at how traditional religious leaders—men who had the reputation of being spiritual leaders and even mystics—were satisfied with words, thoughts, concepts. I thought at first that surely these leaders were quite justifiably concealing from me, a mere outsider, the hidden practical side of their discipline. As I have already mentioned, the whole idea of spiritual reserve or secrecy was taking on a new importance to me. Yet now, sitting across from Father Vassilios, I had for a moment the same unpleasant feeling I experienced throughout my trip—that the only secrets left in Christianity were yet more words and thoughts.

Father Vassilios was not at all surprised. He was quite aware that Westerners were learning about Orthodoxy through two or three books that centered around the prayer of Jesus. I saw him searching for a way to reply to an American's—or a nonbeliever's—lack of comprehension. Finally, he answered me at great length on the subject of grace and its relationship to emotion. He spoke of the Jesus prayer as a form of worship and said that all worship requires sincerity and humility. Purity of feeling could not come through anything but the acceptance of the blood of Christ.

I cannot here convey the intensity with which he spoke—I mean to say the quality of attention that he compelled from me by the evenness of his thought.

I felt warmed by the tremendous effort he was obviously making to communicate to me. I began to grasp the teachings of Orthodox Christianity in a way that had never before been possible for me. In the long silences I watched the darkness settling in the room and enjoyed the balmy night wind that began to blow off the sea. But during these silences there were several moments when I glancingly observed something important take place in myself: I saw the believer in myself begin to arise and step forward.

Let me say at once that concerning the *faith* of which Jesus Christ spoke I know nothing, and it is not this that I am now speaking of. What I saw in myself I have seen many times before and I have seen it in others—indeed I have sometimes succeeded, not to my credit, in provoking it in others. If I call it belief, or the believer, I do not mean to limit it only to the religious sphere, though surely it is in that sphere that it is the most insidious in its action.

I do not think it is necessary here to attempt a psychological description of this process. Suffice it to say that this belief has the taste of inner violence about it. It is connected with certain kinds of emotional stress and the wish to resolve this stress, combined with a tiny, ephemeral element of intellectual grasp, with personal attractions, with fears of various sorts, and all presenting itself under the banner of "the imperative to choose"—"commitment"—as though any sort of real freedom of choice is possible in this fog of self-deception and hidden fragmentation.

How much of what we often call "religious passion" on the "battleground of the freedom of the will" is really only this state of confusion? What is the real struggle for faith? Don't we flatter ourselves thinking that we are on a level of consciousness in which this struggle is even possible? We very much need to ponder this question, which touches upon one of the most significant ways we have distorted the idea of mercy and catholicity in Christianity, thereby avoiding the recognition that we need help in order to be brought to the ability to choose.

So with Father Vassilios I continued to press the topic of method —searching for another way of putting it so as to get away from the suggestion of a mere technique or manipulative device.

"In all the great traditions," I said, "there seems to be a common idea of mercy or compassion that goes hand in hand with the idea of justice and rigor. But isn't it more than an idea? Aren't there practical expressions of this mercy—and, if so, aren't they based on a precise knowledge of the human organism—the emotional strengths and weaknesses, the influence of the body on the psyche and vice versa?

"To me, it is obvious," I continued, "that many contemporary people feel in Yoga or Zen something that comes closer to mercy in action, even though the word mercy is hardly ever used in comparison with Christianity.

"What I mean is that they feel—to some extent—that the working of their minds and bodies are being understood. Therefore they sense communication being offered. To be helped to sit quietly, to begin to observe directly the transitoriness and gradations of the thoughts that govern our lives: isn't such a thing necessary before or at least at the same time that one exhorts someone to faith?"

I was about to go on in this vein, sweeping aside all my reservations about the way Americans naïvely gobbled up Orientalisms of various sorts. I risked exaggerating the success of Eastern religion in America because I was now sure that Father Vassilios did not fully grasp the need that was being felt in America—in California—for a new quality of psychological experience.

But he interrupted me with a quiet laugh, and startled both me and my interpreter. "I could tell you of things a thousand times better than your Yoga," he said.

Evangelos's eyes opened wide as he momentarily dropped his role of interpreter. He turned his whole body toward Father Vassilios, and my ignorance of Greek did not prevent me from understanding what Evangelos was asking. Father Vassilios answered him a little curtly and then, speaking in French, went on to another topic as though regretting that he had let something slip.

"What did he say?" I asked.

"I asked him what things he was speaking about," said Evangelos, in a state of barely concealed excitement and disappointment. "He answered that he only meant the Jesus prayer and such things. . . ."

The conversation moved on. It was getting quite late; the moon was high and no longer visible through the windows. In the darkness we could barely make out each other's faces.

"Do you believe that tradition ever changes?" I asked. "By tradition, I mean the rituals, the liturgy, the forms. Are not adaptations necessary in the light of changing circumstances, changes in people's problems and habits of living and thinking?"

"The liturgy," said Father Vassilios, "embraces the whole of life from birth . . . or before birth . . . until death. How could it change? It is permanent. Yet, at the same time, it is in constant movement. . . . Within the liturgy a man must find the liturgy within himself. We must become a new being. Every minute a man converts, every instant he becomes Orthodox. . . ."

More and more, as he spoke, my admiration grew for this man's refusal to stand outside Orthodoxy in order to explain it to me. Yet at the same time I began to feel an impulse to bring the conversation down to earth. And so I presumed to interrupt him again. "What about other religions?"

Evangelos phrased my blunt question in such a way that Father Vassilios thought I was asking about ecumenicism.

He took a long time before replying. "The Church must confess, not discuss. Orthodoxy is like Jesus in the world. It has the truth for anyone who wants it. Like Jesus, it says 'I am.' It can do no more. Like Jesus, it says 'Not my will, but Thy will.'"

Father Vassilios leaned forward toward me in the darkness. I could just make out his eyes and the rest of his features. What he then said to me contained such poignancy that it brought all my questioning to an end.

"The Church knows that other teachings are attracting the young. It knows that if it changed certain things, that would not be happening. But it must remain what it is. It does so with tears. It knows that it drives people away."

I waited, and then turned to Evangelos to signal that for my part I had nothing more to ask. But no one moved.

I returned to California with more questions than answers. I had begun my journey wondering what modern man must do to *hear* the teachings of tradition as they were intended to be heard—with that in us which is able to hear them. But just here a great difficulty presents itself. Are the present conditions in which we live such that it is possible to hear these teachings? For it is surely an error to believe that merely by listening to words and experiencing a conversion of feeling we will be able to take in the teachings of the masters in a way that touches the whole of our being. Must not a spiritual teaching reach even further down to us—and *help us to hear?*

Are the teachings a means or an end? A means of listening or an end to be listened to? Of what lasting value would it be were I to "accept" the truth and yet remain ignorant of my inherent tendency to distort the truth? Must there not be a way of presenting sacred ideas which at the same time awakens in man the faculty of listening? Without this "little awakening"—as we may call it—it seems naïve to hope for the great awakening. Without it, I shall unconsciously accept or reject great ideas with the same partiality or violence that I accept or reject all the other ideas, divine or demonic, that the world presents to me. I shall become a "believer" or a "doubter"—and the history of civilization is witness to the fact that even great ideas become a destructive influence when they are used to mask ignorance of ourselves.

It is this "little awakening"—without which nothing is possible—that I believe has been forgotten in Western religion, and this forgetting has generated much of the confusion and mischief of dogmatic religion and modern psychology.

For, consider: I had to travel nearly halfway around the world, and only then, with extraordinary luck, was I able to speak to an exceptional man *under conditions that were the manifestation of an idea.* I offer this as speculation, as my own impression. I cannot speak from certainty. But the long voyage, the anticipation, the physical and financial difficulties, the ambience of Athos—its beauty and repulsiveness (again I am speaking subjectively)—all of this and much else: my particular fatigue, my *need* to understand something, the darkening room, the straining to understand the language, the attempt to read the eyes of Vassilios—I could go on with this guesswork. My point is that I came to understand a fragment of Orthodox Christianity only under conditions that to some extent reflected a true idea about man (myself) as he is and man as he can become, conditions corresponding to the double nature of man, a being partly divine (in his wish for truth) and partly an animal (in his egoistic understanding of it). In any case, in these conditions, I *listened.* I will not even say that I was *able* to listen, only that to some extent listening was able to take place.

I do not know to what extent these conditions were intentional or accidental. I believe it was the latter, but this issue is not central to my question. I am simply saying that I have met many men, some of whom were possibly men of even greater spiritual intelligence and of even greater articulateness than this good Father Vassilios. But, apart from a few very notable exceptions, real listening was never able to take place. All the talk in the world about spiritual methods can no longer obscure, for me, the fact that genuine spiritual method begins with the conditions under which ideas are given and under which they are received.

What little I know of the life of ancient man makes me suspect that under the conditions of life that once existed (and that perhaps still exist in parts of Asia) man was more exposed to both sides of his nature. We may surmise that the external conditions of traditional society contained factors to remind men of what they lose through their egoism—so that even in the midst of man's perversity and brutality, as well as in the midst of his apparent moments of triumph, he was not without the help of a cosmic, universal scale by which to taste directly his insignificance and dependence. Modern writers who hold up the violence or injustice of the past as marks of its inferiority fail to consider that a higher civilization is not necessarily one in which men behave like angels, but in which men can experience *both* their divinity and their animality.

If we understand divine love to be the manifestation of truth on the plane of earth, then surely what we are speaking about here is the establishment of conditions—psychological and physical—that are the manifestation of the truth about man. Nowadays, everyone will agree that verbal and intellectual formulations are only one, and perhaps not the most essential, expression of truth. For example, we see in the symbolism of sacred art the transmission of ideas directly into the emotions of man, into that "heart" that can speak in active voice to the intellect that chooses and is able to attend, to listen to it. Yet perhaps more essential—or, for us, more basic, more necessary—even than art or verbal formulations is the establishment of conditions of living that reflect truth, the truth about ourselves— conditions that make listening possible. Thus the mercy or compassion of a teaching consists not only in the contents it brings but in the conditions under which it brings them. To separate the contents of a teaching from the conditions in which it can be heard can result only in arid scholasticism or blind fanaticism.

In order not to be misunderstood, I wish to make clear something about the meaning of the word "conditions" that is implicit in everything that I have been saying. By stressing the conditions that are necessary for the reception of truth, I do not mean to endorse certain external arrangements, such as robes or communes or rules of conduct, while condemning others. In general, that is how we always tend to look at these things and it has really led us nowhere. We tend to think that external conditions by themselves can be good or bad, useful or harmful.

But that is only dogma in the form not of words but of physical arrangements. Dogmatic ideas are found not only in books but also in the structuring of surroundings, behavior, and rules.

We forget our real inner situation when we think in this way. For we ourselves are such deeply conditioned beings, so passive and suggestible, that no external conditions, however inspired, can by themselves lead us to anything more than new forms of blind dependence. Even inner conditions, such as breathing techniques or special postures of meditation, are not always helpful.

Yet help is necessary. So there is the mystery: how to find that particular angle of vision or inner attitude in which one looks at all things from the perspective of a search for one's own understanding. Merely adding or subtracting outer forms will not automatically produce this attitude.

Here we are in front of a little-noted problem about the struggle for consciousness: external help is possible only to someone who can face the conditions offered from the point of view of a learner. In order to reflect the truth about man, given conditions must contain the demand that we search for this attitude toward ourselves at the very moment of submission to them.

Herein, surely, lies one of the roots of the confusion we suffer from in California and perhaps in the modern world. By themselves, great works of art or true ideas cannot effect real change in man. The energy one receives from ideas or experiences cannot be contained by "fallen" man and serves only further to activate the very weaknesses that made him require these ideas in the first place. Witness the destruction brought about by modern science's hasty application of ideas that in the milieu of past civilizations were reserved for the initiate, or in any case given in a form and under conditions in which men could take them in alongside impressions of their own helplessness and dependence. (I am referring to such ideas as those of the infinite universe and of the idea of human evolution.)* Thus, though the sacred impulse to learn for oneself was the germ of modern science, it rapidly became a destructive influence because of

* This point is developed more fully in my book *A Sense of the Cosmos: The Encounter of Modern Science and Ancient Truth* (New York: Doubleday, 1975).

the conditions of living that prevailed in the modern era, conditions that corresponded to no great truth about man but that only manifested man's excessive desire for comfort and egoistic security.

It has been said that the greatness of Western man lies in his impulse to *act* in accordance with truth, an impulse that receives its supreme expression in the teachings of the Old Testament. We know that in modern times this impulse to act was for one reason or another cut off from the sense of a higher truth. The result has been a haste to promote and apply great ideas not fully digested or understood—again, the disastrous results of scientific technology and various political ideologies are witness to this. Our sorrow is that we do not act from ideas but from our reaction to ideas, reactions that are part of what the Eastern traditions call the "desire-nature" and what Western religion once spoke of as the "carnal body," the flesh. I think this is a basic fact about our present situation and accounts for many of our difficulties. Therefore, if sacred ideas are to be transmitted to us, it must be under conditions that take this fact about our nature into full account. But where shall we find the truth transmitted under conditions that enable us simultaneously to study this fact about ourselves and to witness it in action and therefore to see directly the process by which great ideas are distorted in ourselves and made into their opposite, even while the verbal formulations remain intact? The mere preservation of conceptual formulations, rituals, and sacred texts cannot help if the conditions under which these are given us do not open us at the same time to a direct experience of our distortion process.

The study of the movement between psychological states is therefore a necessity for us. The state of wonder, the sense of the sacred, even the collectedness of the state of meditative silence pass over into ordinary inattention and violence, self-deception and sentimentality, breeding cruelty or resentment or subhuman softness. Where shall we find help to study the process that takes place when, for example, I walk from within the sacred space of a Gothic cathedral (or from the state engendered in me by systems of ideas that are like cathedrals) into the pulls and shocks of twentieth-century life? Is there a teaching that so intimately understands the processes of twentieth-century life that it can create conditions in which this movement, this pull outward and downward from truth into the hypnosis of our era, can be witnessed, studied, and accepted in full? *That*, I suggest, would be compassion.

There are many modern observers of the present American religious scene who praise the increasing hunger for "experience." But do we in America really see what we want from experience? External action seems to have reached its limits in the world around us—the promises of pragmatism are foundering against the crises of environmental destruction, meaningless pleasures, and increased social despair. Is our search for inner experience only the application of the lust for action to the inner life? Are our emotions and thoughts like forests and rivers that we manipulate with the same disastrous love of progress that has brought us to the edge of physical extinction?

In short, not even great spiritual methods brought from authentic sources and preserved intact throughout time can of themselves help us. Nor can great ideas or sacred art. Not just new experiences but wider experiences of ourselves are what we need so that the energy produced by spiritual techniques or great ideas is not squandered in the old ways. And as for these wider experiences of ourselves, of our whole nature as double beings in twentieth-century life: where shall we find the conditions to attract us to such experiences?

I remind you that I speak as a Californian. Yet I suspect that what has been called "Californialand"—a state of confusion mixed with the raw hunger for transcendence—exists throughout the Americanized world. As an inhabitant of "Californialand" I ask of what use would it be were we suddenly to surround ourselves with sacred symbols once again, or even with ancient patterns of community relationship? Without some help that would enable us to touch those deeper layers of feeling in ourselves that can open our eyes to our egoism, which accepts, believes, trusts, and distorts everything, how could traditional patterns of life transform our being?

We are surrounded by countless "new religions." At the same time, teachers from the Orient and the Middle East are struggling to preserve and transmit their own traditions within the frame of Western society, where the political conditions, the affluence, and the emotional needs conspire to offer tolerance to any teaching that brings striking ideas about man or new inner experiences.

But can a teaching, however authoritative, be true for us if it persuades us to exercise a faculty that we do not possess, a faculty that is itself the product of long spiritual work? How many of these "new religions" urge us to accept one set of ideas, to enter into a particular stream of practice, while rejecting others? What is the meaning of the call for choice to men who have no power of real choice?

What is needed, I conclude, is a teaching in which *we are known,* not only for what we can become but for what we are—a teaching that provides us with both experiences of our possibilities and impressions of our actuality, our real egoism, and our possible freedom. Surely the power to choose can be born only when we stand in the center, between these two qualities of experience. And, I feel sure, without our being situated between these two experiences no ideas from whatever sacred source can act as a guide in the struggle for consciousness of self.

I think the central reason modern psychology undermined the established religions of the West was that through psychology we realized that we had not been known. The ideas of Christianity and Judaism were suddenly revealed to be, for us, mere ideals. With the psychologists we finally felt known.

But, as time has shown, not deeply known. Therein lies the disillusionment with modern psychology. The scale was too small against which we measured our failures as men. So that all the self-acceptance in the world (which was the mercy of modern psychology) could not help us, but kept us mired in illusions about ourselves. In attempting to free us from neurotic guilt, psychology only helped us for a time to feel comfortable about ourselves but never to discover the struggle for greater being. The reason for the method of self-acceptance was too small, too egoistic and introverted.

Yet, although it fails by exaggerating the importance of its partial insights about the human personality, modern psychology leaves us with the hope for ideas and methods that can actually work real changes in ourselves. No wonder teachings have now appeared that attempt to connect sacred traditions with the general orientation of modern psychology!

The truth is, we lack the touchstone by which to recognize an authentic path of self-knowledge. The real hiddenness and the real corruption of tradition stems from the ignorance of this fact.

But does this mean we ought to abandon the question how to recognize what knowledge we need? Quite the contrary. It *is* our question, and to deny it is to deny our starting point.

But there is another question, equally fundamental, that must be asked at the same time but that we rarely ask in a serious way. That question is, "What does it mean to learn?"

The first question—that of recognizing authenticity—when taken alone, drives us outward in the effort to experience external reality by our own lights (and is thus the origin of modern science). This movement outward is something dogmatic religion obstructs, even though it wishes to do good by shaping our thought to conform to great ideas. Perhaps there is a place for dogmatic religion in a culture that still allows for the shocks of real experiences—death, physical effort, and the intensity of harmonious sexual experience. But as cultures and nations now interact with an increasingly accidental and violent quality, the experiences available in any modern community tend to become both more uniform and more excessive—overwhelming shocks interspersing the general drift toward ease and self-deception.

In the absence of the necessary real experiences, religious dogma or ill-digested experiences edge man into the wastelands of mental or emotional identity, the closure of thought or feeling around great ideas or experiences that are never understood by the whole person in body and heart.

But the question "What does it mean to learn?" has the power to lead us inward to observe for ourselves what is required if the parts of our inner nature are to come together if only for an instant. A man who realizes that he has never observed this inner process and therefore does not understand or accept the conditions of real learning is in a better position to question the criteria he sets up for a teacher or a teaching. Without asking this question, without realizing that we do not know what great learning demands of us, we abandon ourselves merely to finding a teaching with "credentials."

We need to acknowledge that there are two kinds of learning—one given, as is said, by life and the other by books. Even the previous generation maintained this distinction, which has played an important role in American life and has been one of the factors that distinguished American life, for all its faults, from that of the more sophisticated European civilization. But the present generation in this country has obliterated even that weakened version of the distinction between what a man learns with the whole of himself and what he learns only with his mind—that is to say, what he takes in as material for the growth of a new consciousness and what he takes in for utilitarian reasons of comfort, psychological safety, or physical pleasure.

The new generation of Americans who have been captured by drugs, encounter groups, Eastern religion, or the Jesus movement have this one thing in common with the generation that precedes them: all were raised and educated by a system that tried to consider both emotional and mental factors as part of ordinary learning. Up until rather recent times, modern civilization, for all its anti-traditionalism, left the development of the emotional life to the family. The mother's role in this was of overwhelming importance. A person had to find himself somewhere in between his mother and the shocks of life. The place of the father was as a representative of aspiration. Mother and father therefore had the task of preparing a person to grow in the midst of life and not to forget God. In this respect, regarding the subtle uniqueness of feeling that arises in the child and that can be maintained through adolescence only with the support of a family reality containing in some measure the aspiration of man, the family was always the first spiritual teacher, or in any event the preparer of the psyche for the spiritual teacher.

The spread of public education and the growth of psychoanalysis and other psychological theories resulted in the mixing of book learning with emotional training sometimes explicitly carried out by educational theorists and often carried out by schoolteachers who themselves believed in the theories of the psychologists.

Public emotional training placed the emphasis on connecting feelings and performance, assuming that feelings were for the support of the ego rather than a special and irreplaceable access to a higher intelligence. The uniqueness of feeling was drowned out by the noise of general emotional training. As a result, the most essential element of real learning was completely forgotten in modern culture: namely, that man can learn from life only to the extent that he can accept the suffering such learning demands.

What sort of suffering? This is a difficult question that cannot be answered merely from theory. I believe that almost everyone, if he tries, can remember in his life an occasion when he turned away from the process of deep learning. Perhaps it was in the moment of a grievous shock such as the death of a loved one, or when abruptly awakening to oneself in the midst of awesome nature or overwhelming physical pain, or when dealt the sort of sudden personal disappointment that pulls out from under one's feet all the illusions about life that support our sense of direction.

In those moments, for a fleeting second, a voice can sometimes be heard within us that comes from a world we never knew existed. In those moments we see that there are actually two levels of reality within our nature. We sometimes describe this experience by saying that everything seemed unreal. But that is not exact. Closer to the truth is that for an instant I realize that this voice is always speaking and that it is I who continually turn away from it. In those exceedingly rare moments, when I am present to the two consciousnesses within my nature, I see that it is not the world that is unreal—it is myself who am a lie. And then, so swiftly that I do not even notice, I am willingly absorbed by all the smaller voices—all the forces of ordinary life—and I "come back to myself."

It would be quite wrong to think of such moments as "peak experiences" or "mystical visions." They are nothing of the kind. But surely, without them, without accepting what they teach us about ourselves, and without the help we require in order to find our way to them more often, not even great ideas or ancient spiritual techniques can change our lives. For, without this acceptance of our blindness to the two natures within us, the living knowledge of the great traditions will fall upon a consciousness that eternally crucifies the truth upon the cross of our unseen egoism.

Into the present milieu many traditional teachers bring ideas, doctrines, and methods of the past, speaking to men and women who do not know what it means to learn and who, because of the disintegration of the family, do not have access to subtle feeling and who therefore trust only the egoistic emotions which are the by-product of the hopeless struggle for mental or emotional identity. Teachers who come to America from more traditional surroundings seem unaware of how far this process has gone here in the West and are perhaps deceived by the apparent willingness of thousands to listen to them.

As I see it, therefore, it is not the content of our beliefs that makes us an antitraditional society, or even the forms of our behavior. It is rather the ease with which we ignore the distinction between two kinds of learning—so much so that the deeper learning, the reception of real experiences for the sake of forging inward connections between the vast scales of reality that exist in man, is forgotten. And with it is forgotten the possible evolution of man as a being between two worlds.

Christianity in Dialogue
with Zen

William Johnston, S.J.

. . .
.

IT IS a good question: Can the ancient religions speak to modern man? Have they anything meaningful to say? For who can doubt that Western man is searching? Isolated, alienated, and fearful, he asks questions about life and death, about human identity, about suffering, about meaning, about the use of his new-found liberty. He is characterized (Dr. Needleman has told us) by "an intensive search for the transcendent." And his almost frantic search manifests itself not only in profound studies of philosophy and psychology and the social sciences but even more strikingly in encounter groups, in meditation, in drug experimentation, in interest in Oriental arts. Modern man explores altered states of consciousness; he analyzes his dreams; he looks for new possibilities in human relationships. In recent times there is scarcely a newspaper or magazine that has not featured some article or series of articles on modern man's *search*.

And in the midst of all the restlessness and dissatisfaction it becomes clear that Western man yearns for guidance and for the *guru*. Beneath a façade of talk about liberation, equality, and democracy, he is like a lost and lonely child crying out for someone to show him the way. Does Christianity have any guidance to offer? Can she play the role of the guru?

At first sight it might seem that not only Christianity but all the traditional religions fit into the category of lost causes. Religions that at one time gave inspiration to art and music and poetry; religions that were the guardians of education and the spokesmen in political life—these same religions now find themselves confronted with secularized art, secularized music and poetry, secularized politics, secularized education, and a secularized world. Most surprising of all, in recent times they find themselves confronted with secularized prayer. For in the modern world we have seen the rise of a great meditation movement seemingly divorced from religion and geared to the development of human potential. If there is one activity that traditional religion might confidently claim as its own, surely it is meditation. Yet even here traditional religion seems to have lost its grip. We find meditators who are neither Christian nor Buddhist nor Jew nor Hindu but simply meditators and searchers. What a blow to the ancient religions!

Almost fifty years ago Alfred North Whitehead saw the problem. Both Christianity and Buddhism, he claimed, had lost their influence; and the root cause of their decline was *their reluctance to dialogue*. For the believer his words hold a certain poignancy:

> The decay of Christianity and Buddhism, as determinative influences in modern thought, is partly due to the fact that *each religion has unduly sheltered itself* from the other. The self-sufficient pedantry of learning and the confidence of ignorant zealots have combined to shut up each religion in its own forms of thought. Instead of looking to each other for deeper meanings, *they have remained self-satisfied and unfertilized* [italics mine].
>
> Both have suffered from the rise of the third tradition, which is science, because neither of them had retained the requisite flexibility of adaptation. Thus the real, practical problems of religion have never been adequately studied in the only way in which such problems *can* be studied; namely, in the school of experience.[1]

Whitehead is clear. If Christianity and Buddhism have lost their influence, it is because rigid and narrow-minded zealots have refused to dialogue.

Whitehead's words were written in 1926; and in the 1960s the world-wide Catholic Church came to a somewhat similar conclusion. Catholicism had been too much the beseiged city or the beleaguered castle. It had unduly sheltered itself from contemporary thought and from other religions. It must get out of the Middle Ages to enter into dialogue with the rest of mankind. It must mature, grow, develop. Such was the message of Vatican II. "The Church therefore has this exhortation for her sons: Prudently and lovingly, through dialogue and collaboration with the followers of other religions, and in witness of Christian faith and life, acknowledge, preserve, and promote the spiritual and moral goods found among these men, as well as the values in their society and culture."[2]

[1] Alfred North Whitehead, *Religion in the Making* (Cambridge, England, 1926), pp. 146–47.
[2] *Declaration on the Relationship of the Church to Non-Christian Religions,* Section 2.

Whitehead, had he been alive, might well have smiled. The intolerant Catholic Church was at last opening windows and doors, letting in the fresh air, listening humbly to other people, issuing a clarion call to dialogue.

And yet these ideas of Vatican II were by no means as revolutionary as might at first appear. From its very beginnings Christianity was committed to an ongoing dialogue which admittedly was less conspicuous in the rigid years between Trent and Vatican II. Starting as a Jewish religion, founded by a Jew, and proud of its Jewish origins, Christianity was destined to break out of its Hebrew framework through dialogue with a Hellenistic world. And, interesting to note, this dialogue was initiated and ardently promoted by a Jew, a Hebrew of the Hebrews, Paul of Tarsus. "You cannot make the Gentiles live like Jews!" he exclaimed angrily to Saint Peter; and he spent much of his burning energy in promoting the universal dimension of the risen Jesus whom he loved. So it was that there came into existence a Hellenistic Christianity. The men who built the Western Church were Hellenistic in background and education— Augustine, Gregory I, Bernard of Clairvaux, Aquinas, and the rest.

Hellenism contributed vastly to the enrichment of the Western Church. The insights of Plato and Aristotle and Plotinus, and even of Homer and Virgil, gave life and energy to the schoolmen and the artists of the Middle Ages. But one can always have too much of a good thing, and cockle is usually sown amidst the wheat. Catholic theologians now feel (and rightly, I believe) that Catholic Christianity got an overdose of Hellenism. Thanks to a Greek way of thinking, theology tended to categorize, to see things neatly, to conceptualize, to rationalize. And, alas, in the years after Trent, *growth stopped*. Or it almost stopped. Christianity in both its Catholic and Protestant forms became incapable of opening itself to other cultures. Great missionaries such as Robert de Nobili in India and Mateo Ricci in China who attempted to enter into serious dialogue with Eastern religions were sadly reduced to silence. The inability of Christianity to recognize the beauty and validity of the Chinese rites is a tragic episode in her history.

Together with Vatican II and the end of the post-Reformation period, however, came a purification of Christianity from Hellenistic exaggeration and a return to the biblical sources. And now we see a world-wide Christian Church preparing for a second great dialogue: the dialogue with Oriental religions and culture. This will surely be even more earth-shaking and even more enriching than the Judaeo-Hellenistic encounter. Where it will lead no one knows. But it has begun and nothing can hold it back.

The decrees of Vatican II had a profound influence on the Church in Japan. In some ways they sanctioned work that had already begun. Some more broad-minded missionaries were already searching for the good and the beautiful in Buddhism. The ideas and ideals of Ricci had not been forgotten. Attempts were being made to learn from the methodology of Zen. Some missionaries, devoting themselves to Buddhist studies, had published scholarly works that were acclaimed with enthusiasm by Buddhists. But it is also true that their insights had not been integrated into Christianity. Popular Christianity and popular Buddhism had succeeded in sheltering themselves from one another with all the ingenuity that Whitehead describes. Now, with the Council, things began to change and a new era was ushered in. Christians and Buddhists began to talk, to exchange ideas, to help one another, and the dialogue (called by Toynbee the most significant event in the history of our day) was on.

I myself had the privilege of taking part in the dialogue with Zen. Assuredly this is not the most significant part of the over-all dialogue (for Buddhism is bigger than Zen), but it is one of the more vital areas of exchange. We came together for one week—Zen Buddhists of the Soto and Rinzai sects with Protestants, Catholics, Quakers—searching for common goals and common ideals. Determined that this would be no academic exercise but a real experience, we held a Bible service conducted by the Protestants; we assisted at a Catholic eucharistic celebration; and together we sat cross-legged in Zen. In the discussions that followed we tried to keep the rules of dialogue, avoiding apologetics and controversy. We did not try to convert one another; nor did we endeavor to defend a position. No one was asked to compromise his beliefs or convictions. Rather, we *explained* and shared. We spoke mainly about our own religious experience and its meaning for our lives. This, we thought, was more meaningful than philosophical and theological discussion. All in all it was a fascinating meeting. It initiated a dialogue that still goes on.

It became clear to me that the great religions are organic and dynamic. That is to say, far from being collections of static teaching, they are still growing and changing and developing. As the human race evolves and moves toward maturity, its religions move with it.

This organic growth is particularly evident in the Hebrew-Christian tradition. The Old Testament relates the growth of a people and the development of its understanding of Yahweh and his ways. With the New Testament comes further development: the vision of a human race guided by the Spirit and moving toward the second coming of Christ, the eschatological point of convergence which Teilhard de Chardin has called "Christ Omega." As it moves forward (and in order to move forward) Christianity dialogues with Marxism, with existentialism, with secularism, with Buddhism, with Hinduism, with Judaism. But at the same time it must remain faithful to its past—to its founder and his gospel. Indeed, fidelity to the past is both a condition for, and an incentive to, growth. As in the growth of any human being, Christianity is faced with the task of integrating the old and the new in each succeeding stage of development. To cut off the past would be a disaster: to cling to the past retards all growth.

And so I came to the conclusion that the ancient religions will not satisfy modern man *if they remain ancient*. But they need not and, I believe, will not remain ancient. Like any other organism they have the potentiality to grow to maturity while remaining true to their past.

Returning to the dialogue with Zen, I would like to discuss three points of interest: first, the common ground where Zen and traditional Christian meditation (or contemplation) are at one; second, the unique and valuable contributions of Zen; and third, the unique and valuable contributions of traditional Christianity. Since the dialogue has only begun I cannot say the last word on these points; but I can share some of my insights.

First of all, the common ground. This is found mainly in the area of experience. Zen practitioners and Christian contemplatives find themselves doing something very similar on the practical level. No doubt this is because of a common human nature, a common humanity, a common psychology. They enter a whole new area of human consciousness characterized by nonconceptual (or, more correctly, transconceptual) awareness. This is a state of quiet, of emptiness, of silence, of unification—and the Christian form is characterized by an obscure sense of presence. It is a state in which one ignores the stream of consciousness that passes across the surface of the mind, because one is unified at a deeper level of psychic life. It has been compared to "the cloud of unknowing" into which Moses entered when he climbed the mountain to receive the Ten Commandments from Yahweh. This state is the silent nothingness of the Japanese *mu*, the emptiness of the Spanish *nada*. It is a kind of meditation that Western man now searches for. Wearied with reasoning and thinking and conceptualization, he longs for deeper states of consciousness in which he can find peace. Yet this is an area in which he needs guidance, because the journey into the caverns of the mind is a serious undertaking, fraught with peril and psychological hazards. It is not possible to discuss these here. Sufficient to say that the ancient traditions have much to offer in the way of practical experience and guidelines. Western man can learn a great deal from the Zen master as well as from the traditional teaching of *The Cloud of Unknowing, The Book of Privy Counselling,* and the works of Saint Teresa of Avila.

Since I have mentioned supraconceptual thinking, let me digress for a moment to mention one outstanding characteristic of Christian guidance in this area. While the orthodox Christian writers lead their disciples *beyond* reason, they never *reject* reason. Christianity has always eschewed the cult of irrationality and has felt that dogma—whatever its problems—is a safeguard in the venture into deeper states of consciousness. And so, though in the prayer of quiet one abandons reasoning and thinking and imagery in favor of a deeper, intuitive level of awareness, outside the time of meditation and in helping to direct it, reason and dogma have important parts to play. The notion of "going beyond reason" is very central to a correct understanding of Christian contemplation.

A second point on which Zen and Christian contemplation find common ground is the stress on nonattachment. Both systems tell us to "let go" of all things in order to enter "the cloud of unknowing." This letting go is apparent in the numerous magnificent statues of the Buddha, with their ethereal calm and compassion and wisdom. It is clear also in Saint John of the Cross, who says that attachment is like the thread around the leg of the little bird, hindering its flight into the clear, blue sky—we must break the thread of clinging attachment in order to fly in the way of wisdom. And the greatest attachment is toward one's self. Self (say both systems) must be lost—as Jesus says that we must lose our false self to find our true self. The best modern psychology seems to support this teaching of a detachment that humanizes and leads to love and compassion; but here again modern man needs guidance. For the fact is that nonattachment brings inevitable suffering and purificatory dark nights. What terrible anguish there is in the loss of one ego and the finding of the next! What agonizing insecurity in falling into nothingness until one finds one's true self! And then, nonattachment is so easily misunderstood, so easily confused with self-destruction. Without guidance people can go astray or get discouraged or be subjected to unnecessary suffering. I doubt if the would-be meditator can get all the help he needs from psychologists such as Carl Jung and Abraham Maslow (brilliant and admirable though they may be); he had better look to the store of wisdom contained in the ancient traditions.

A third point in common is the great joy that accompanies meditation, be it Christian or Buddhist. It is as though a certain unconscious force is unleashed from the depths of one's being, reaching its peak in the ecstatic delight of enlightenment. Radical and all-pervading, this joy is paradoxically present in the midst of darkness. Hence the paradox of joy and anguish found in both traditions of meditation.

These are just a few points in which Zen and Christian contemplation share common ground. More could be mentioned. But what has been said may show a similarity in psychological process. Both are paths of joy, of suffering, of silence, of darkness, leading to a great enlightenment (be it sudden or gradual) and the opening up of new levels of awareness. In the great religious traditions we find centuries, even millennia, of accumulated wisdom regarding this meditational path. Surely here is powerful guidance for modern man.

What can Zen give to Christian meditation?

First of all, Christianity can learn (and is learning) from the eminent practicality of Zen. When the aspirant comes asking for guidance, Zen can teach him to sit in the lotus posture, to be quiet, to deepen his awareness. And modern neurophysiological studies have sanctioned the value of these techniques for bringing people into the state of relaxed awareness characterized by the high-amplitude brain wave. Then there is the whole methodology of Zen—not only the bodily posture but the order of time during the retreat or *sesshin*, the diet that is most conducive to deep concentration and awareness, the early rising, the assiduous sitting, the "walking Zen," and all the rest. This would be of particular value to Western monasticism, now searching for renewal and reform.

For, one great contribution of the East to a new mysticism is surely its stress upon the body and the notion that the body itself can pray. While Western meditation goes to the intuitive through the rational (through reasoning and thinking), Eastern meditation can teach us to go to the intuitive through the body. The very fact of sitting in the lotus can be an act of adoration. Not that this notion of "the praying body" is entirely absent from the West. The Semitic tradition (in which Christianity is rooted) had no problem about the body-soul dichotomy; but in the later Hellenistic centuries in the West the role of the body in meditation was greatly neglected except in movements such as Hesychasm, where posture and the control of the breathing were central for "the prayer of Jesus" or "the prayer of the heart."

Again, the West can profit from the Zen method of direction. The Zen masters have a remarkable grasp of the working of the human mind in meditation and they have an outstanding technique for leading their disciples to enlightenment.

But the great contribution that the West can make to the future of meditation and mysticism in the world is its notion of personality: the personality of man and the personality of ultimate reality or God. I call this a contribution of "the West" because it is not only Christian but also Hebrew and Greek. It is to the Hebrew tradition that the world owes its knowledge of an ultimate reality with a name: Yahweh. For Aristotle ultimate reality is *Mind*, "the thought that thinks itself"; and in the New Testament the vocation of Jesus is to reveal the Father.

Now belief in personality makes a great difference to meditation. This does not mean that during meditation one thinks about persons (this would destroy the imageless silence of the exercise) but rather that one sits in the lotus open in the core of his being to a wisdom he knows to be personal. He believes that as he searches for wisdom, wisdom searches for him. In the depth of his heart he believes that "God is faithful" or that "God is love"; or he is motivated by the words, "Let us love God because God has first loved us." All this transforms his meditation, making it intensely human and intensely personal without robbing it of imageless silence and deep emptiness. Teilhard de Chardin profoundly distinguishes between mysticism that dissolves personality in general cosmic consciousness and mysticism that realizes a higher personalism. The latter is the mysticism of the West. Again he distinguishes between *absorption*, in which self is lost, and *union*, which differentiates in such ways that I become my true self in oneness with the other. Western mysticism ends up in the terrible paradox that one becomes the other while remaining oneself—and this is because of the belief in personality.

In Christianity meditation is rendered all the more personal by the role of Christ, with whom the meditator is identified while remaining himself. "I live, now not I, but Christ liveth in me," cried Paul; and his words have been echoed by countless mystics through the centuries. It is the Spirit of Jesus within who (to quote Paul again) "joins himself to our spirit and calls out 'Abba, Father!'" In this way Christ, present at the level of the true self, is calling to the Father—and we find ourselves in a Trinitarian experience where all is one, yet all is not one.

When we speak of *person*, however, a word of caution must be thrown in. The *personal* nature of ultimate reality, the personal nature of the risen Christ—this must not be confused with anthropomorphism. The personal Christ of whom the mystics speak is, in Teilhard's words, a "superperson" or a "transperson" of whom the human persons we meet are but pale reflections. Mysticism is an encounter and union with the cosmic Christ of the universe who lives at the heart of matter, a greater reality than that which immediately meets our physical gaze. Nor is this pantheism. It is simply Saint Paul's Christology, which sees the risen Jesus as the head of the entire creation, "seated at the right hand of the Father." And we, as his members, live, move, and have our being in him. All this is of the greatest importance for the meditator. An undue tendency to anthropomorphism, a tendency to think of ultimate reality in terms of purely human personality, would destroy all mysticism—which necessarily goes beyond forms and images and thoughts to the deepest level of awareness. To think of Christ in his purely historical form without the realization that this same Christ has become cosmic and imageless through resurrection would detract from the depths of the mystical experience.

Grasping this, we can understand why, in certain schools of the Western tradition, mysticism is nothing other than a love affair with the Christ of the universe. This way of thinking goes back not only to John and Paul but even further to the Canticle, to Hosea, to Isaiah, to Ezekiel, where Yahweh is the bridegroom and the people are the bride. With Bernard of Clairvaux, the author of *The Cloud of Unknowing*, Saint John of the Cross, and the rest, it is Christ, the risen Christ who is now the bridegroom. "Seeking my love," writes Saint John of the Cross, "I will head for the mountains. I will gather no flowers; I will fear no wild beasts"—as if to say that neither seductive flowers nor the yawning mouths of wild animals will deter him from the search for the one he loves. And of the ultimate union he writes:

> Just as in the consummation of carnal marriage there are two in one flesh, as Sacred Scripture points out (Genesis 2:24), so also when the spiritual marriage between God and the soul is consummated, there are two natures in one spirit and love, as Saint Paul says in making this same comparison: "He who is joined to the Lord is one spirit with Him" (I Corinthians 6:17). This union resembles the union of the light of a star or candle with the light of the sun, for what then sheds light is not the star or the candle, but the sun, which has absorbed the other lights into its own.[3]

Here we see at once a remarkable loss of self and a certain "Christian pantheism" together with a union in personalities that can be compared to marriage. And, again, this love affair is nowhere more evident than in the life of the scientist mystic Teilhard de Chardin, whose burning love for matter and for the world and for man was a way to, and an expression of, his great love for the cosmic Christ. And it should be noted that this love is not simply devotional or emotional *bhakti* but a love that burns at the deepest level of the person, at the level where the most profound *satori* comes to birth.

From this we can draw several conclusions. One is that Christian mysticism is necessarily incarnational. Far from being a flight from matter into some world of pure spirit, it is a deeper penetration into matter and into the universe, where one discovers the cosmic Christ. Saint Teresa of Avila kept insisting that the mystic must never deliberately abandon the humanity of Christ, however lofty and spiritual his aspirations. By this she meant the risen Christ, the center of the cosmos that lies before our eyes. The conviction that the Spirit of the risen Christ permeates the world of matter and moves forward the thrust of evolution leads necessarily to esteem for material progress, esteem for life, and confidence in the future.

A second conclusion is that authentic Christian mysticism neces-

3 *The Collected Works of St. John of the Cross*, trans. by Kieran Kavanagh and Otilio Rodriguez (Washington, D.C.: ICS Publications, 1973), p. 497.

sarily leads to love of man and to deep interpersonal relations. From a loving interpersonal relationship with Christ comes love and intimacy with men who are the members of Christ's body. Love for Christ can never be divorced from love of men with whom Christ is always identified. Hence the whole social dimension of Christian mysticism, hence the dimension of friendship. I would hazard the affirmation that there have been no greater friendships than those between the great Christian mystics. I would hazard the affirmation that these have had the greatest social sense—an empathy with the sick, the suffering, and the anguished of the whole world.

A third conclusion (and this is something that Christianity holds in common with other great religions, and so we are back to common ground) is that authentic mysticism is never a search for states of consciousness, increased awareness, sudden illumination, trance, delectable experiences, and all the rest. These things are there—present in abundance. Certainly there are illuminations and experiences of ecstatic joy. But they are never sought for themselves. They are a consequence of something else. In Christianity they are a consequence of faith in Christ and his revelation of the Father. The eyes are fixed on One who lives beyond all categories in the cloud of unknowing. I believe that the traditional Christian tendency to discount and minimize the delectable experiences of mysticism is of primary importance for the meditation movement that is alive in the world today. For one of the great snares and aberrations is surely the search for "kicks," delectable experiences, earth-shaking *satoris*. All such craving is in the end self-defeating and dehumanizing—because man is made for more than "kicks."

In a series of lesser-known essays,[4] Teilhard de Chardin writes of the emergence of a new spirituality and a new mysticism in the contemporary world. The mysticism of the future, he claims, will be quite different from anything we have known: it will be a mysticism of man involved in the world of matter and engaged in building the earth. Many elements will go to make up this world-orientated "mysticism of convergence," but it will be primarily a prolongation of what Teilhard calls "the way of the West." This is because the West has put its emphasis on *being* rather than on *nonbeing*; it has endeavored not to suppress matter but to sublimate it.

It is true that Teilhard, no Orientalist and no specialist in Eastern

[4] See Pierre Teilhard de Chardin, *Les Directions de l'Avenir* (Paris, 1973).

religions, is known for his excessive confidence in the superiority of Western thought. Nevertheless he may here have an insight of some value. It may be that the West can still make a great contribution to the future of mysticism. Quite certainly the last decade has seen in the West a development and expansion of consciousness that is quite remarkable. And beneath a veneer of Oriental externals, the meditation movement that has spread rapidly throughout Europe and America may well have its roots in the traditional psyche of the West. It may ultimately be a Western movement unconsciously engaged in profound dialogue with the East. Perhaps the dialogue with the East, carried on implicitly and unconsciously by giants such as Teilhard, is now rising to the surface of consciousness in the simple East-West meetings in Tokyo and Benares and throughout the world. Such meetings may well be the road signs guiding Western man into the future.

QUESTIONS AND ANSWERS

Q: *I was interested in your suggestion that one contribution Christianity might make in meditation is to stress the idea of a personality, a deeper personal reality, with which one seeks contact in meditation. Is there something you have experienced which would suggest some actual verification of this idea of the Person?*

JOHNSTON: *It's quite common in Christian meditation—and, I believe, in Judaism—to have the experience of being called by name. Now, this being called by name, which people sometimes experience in deep meditation, is not your literal name, John or James; it involves a deeper level of awareness that is only meant to be suggested by expressing it in that way. In the Old Testament you have "Abraham! Abraham!"—or whatever the name might be. This doesn't mean that the person heard his name just the way you're hearing my voice. It means a very deep locution, a deep experience in which you are called. This is a personal encounter in which one has the experience of being loved. And I believe it is an archetypal experience that is found in all the religions, but not in quite the personal way.*

Q: *Do you think there is a parallel in Christian mysticism to the method of the Zen koan?*

JOHNSTON: *I think the Scriptures are full of koans. For instance, Christ says, "Let the dead bury their dead and come follow me." This is a koan. And in First Corinthians, Paul speaks about the crucifixion, describing it as nonsense to Jew and Gentile alike, which means everybody. But if you understand it, it's wisdom. The koan is just that. It appears like nonsense; but once you grasp it, it's wisdom. In fact, in His way of acting, Christ often resembles a Zen master— as when he strikes people in the face, not literally, but metaphorically. "Render unto Caesar the things that are Caesar's, and unto God the things that are God's." Western exegetes have expended a great deal of energy trying to decipher such sayings, but I think Christ was speaking koans.*

Q: *If someone were to ask your advice on how to begin meditation and had never experienced being called by name and did not have faith in God, how could you help them begin?*

JOHNSTON: *Now this is something we Christians learned from Zen and which is really quite beautiful. Before we met Zen, before we began this dialogue with Zen, we felt that people couldn't meditate unless they first believed in God and in many other things as well. But you find with the Zen people that the first thing they teach you is how to sit. They give you the cushion, they teach you the cross-legged position, and they say, "We'll talk later, but the first thing you do is you just sit." I believe this is a very good thing. Never mind what a person believes; it's enough that he's searching, looking. In fact we have a Christian house in Tokyo where we now do just that. We have a group of Christians who sit and meditate in the lotus position, doing zazen in a Christian atmosphere. But if people come and want to join us, we don't demand that they believe in God or anything else. We just say "Come and sit." And when they learn how to sit and how to be conscious of their body, then they learn something, they discover something—so that where previously I used to think of meditation as an exercise of faith, I now also look on it as a search.*

Q: *Do you believe that Christianity can use the Zen idea of a teacher?*

JOHNSTON: *Maybe it can, though not in such a radical way as Zen. Christianity believes very much in the guidance of the Spirit, and in a community, and in not interfering too much. But I think there* is something like this in Zen as well. In fact, the notion of master and disciple is very strong in Christian history, starting with Christ and his disciples. In Buddhism it is sometimes said that the disciple who does not go beyond his master is not worthy of his master. And Christ says to his disciples, "He that believes in me, the things I do, he shall do and greater shall he do, because I go to the Father." He will send the Spirit. So there was certainly the same master-disciple relationship in the case of Christ himself. Christianity has to find its way back to that relationship. But I doubt that it would be the same as it is in Zen. For example, in Zen it is more a case of something being handed down from one person to another and, if I am not mistaken, there's much more in the Zen tradition of obtaining the enlightenment directly from the master than there would be in Christianity. But this is an area that has to be probed and searched a great deal more than has been done.

Q: In the dialogue with Zen what is to be learned about the meaning of suffering?

JOHNSTON: That depends upon what you mean by "suffering." The Zen Buddhists say that you don't come to enlightenment if you have an easy life: you have to pay the price. A Buddhist monk once told me that his greatest moments of enlightenment came when he was hungry and cold during an intense period of meditation—when the body was more or less in bad shape, so to speak. This is very interesting, because Victor Frankl had rather similar experiences in a German concentration camp. In deep religious experience, suffering has a value, I think, because it brings about a certain nonattachment and gives way to the arising of spirit. But in Christianity you have something else as well, where Saint Paul speaks of glorying in the cross of Christ, for love of Christ. And the Old Testament—particularly in Isaiah—speaks of a suffering for the entire universe. And so, I believe that the approach to suffering in Christianity is somehow stronger than in Zen.

Q: Do you feel that institutionalized Christianity is helping the masses of people become enlightened? And if not, what do you think institutionalized religion could do to bring this about?

JOHNSTON: In any institution there are some things that more or less lag behind. However, in institutionalized Christianity the very powerful element leading to enlightenment is the sacraments, especially the Mass. In Buddhism what is called samadhi is the deep sense of silence, of oneness, a deeper level of awareness. Now, on one occasion, we celebrated a Catholic Mass and we were all standing around the altar. Among us was a Buddhist monk. After the Eucharist we all sat down suddenly enshrouded in silence. When I spoke to the monk afterward I said to him that in Catholic Christianity people enter into samadhi mainly through the Eucharist. And he answered, "Yes, I noticed that." He had felt it himself. So, I don't think that institutionalized Christianity crushes mysticism and enlightenment. I would say, instead, that there is an awful lot of ignorance and a great many people who don't know what mysticism and enlightenment are. But I think the tools are there, the possibility of leading people to enlightenment is there. I grant that institutionalized Christianity, both in its Protestant and Catholic form, is not yet meeting this challenge. But I believe it can.

Q: You said that Buddhism doesn't talk in terms of a personal God. But do you feel that Buddhism and Christianity simply use different words for the same thing, or that there is some essential difference between them?

JOHNSTON: First of all, the Buddhist tends not to speak about God at all. However, there is also a trend in Christianity, the theology of negation, that insists we really can't say much about God. In general, I think that Christians have talked too much about God—"I can tell you why he created the world and why he allowed suffering, and so on. Just ask me and I'll tell you." Ridiculous! We can't do that. Buddhism is not like that, not so clear-cut and ready with answers. There are books in Catholic theology where everything is cut and dry, all the answers are given. There's no such book in Buddhism. Perhaps some Buddhists, including some deeply enlightened Buddhists, believe in something like a personal God; but it is not common. And certainly, if a Buddhist were to say he believed in God in the Christian sense this would not be orthodox, at least not in Zen. But if you ask whether we're ultimately saying the same thing, well—we're groping toward something similar. We Christians have too easily accepted the impression that I am here and God is there: I who am here talking to God who is there. But that's to limit God, to put him in a place and to say if he's there then he is not here. And if you tell a Buddhist, "I am here and God is there and I talk to God," then the Buddhist will say, "No God, I don't believe in

God." And that is because there is a tremendous sense of unity in Buddhism. However, if we were to speak of God as ultimate Reality, the center of things, the deepest part of man, the deepest thing in the universe, and say that this is a Person, then we're coming nearer to a common ground with Buddhism.

Q: I have experienced a particular sterility and lack of mystical experience in the Eucharist as it is practiced in both the Catholic and Episcopal Church. I would like to know what changes you might suggest in the approach to the Eucharist so that it would lend itself more toward mysticism or an atmosphere of meditation.

JOHNSTON: Let me return to the Buddhist monk I was speaking about. I said to him that the time Christians were most likely to enter samadhi was after the reception of the Eucharist. But then I added that nowadays they sometimes sing hymns after the Eucharist. "Oh," he said, "that's cutting your own throats." In other words, you should be silent. Whether he was right or not, I can't say— perhaps there should be longer periods of silence. But the point is that if someone actually believes in the divine in-dwelling, that I am Christ and Christ is in me, it is certainly something quite mystical and can lead to the loss of self that Paul speaks of: "I live; yet not I, but Christ liveth in me." So I think the raw material is there in the forms, and perhaps it's only a question of change in liturgy, of more silence and more sense of union.

Q: In Christianity wasn't the higher knowledge contained in the liturgy? And isn't the problem one of understanding this liturgy through meditation?

JOHNSTON: I don't know what you mean when you say that the higher knowledge is in the liturgy. Enlightenment is a thing that must be in people, isn't that so? It's something that people experience. I would say that liturgy is a Way, a tao. And meditation is a Way, too. And both of these things are necessary: the liturgy, the external thing, and this internal meditation—both together.

Q: You spoke of three traditions: the Buddhist, the Christian, and the scientific. My impression is that the Buddhist tradition speaks more about the individual effort, while the Christian tradition speaks of a kind of effort that is being made by an external force to reach me. The scientific tradition seems also to be rooted in the idea of individual discovery, individual search. Then how can Christianity as you've described it have some impact on the scientific tradition, which does exert such a fantastic influence on the way we all think?

JOHNSTON: I'll give you a concrete example. In Tokyo I have been working with a Japanese neurophysiologist who is writing a book on the psychophysiology of Zen. He has had numerous Zen masters in his laboratory, testing their alpha waves, their breathing, their whole physiology. This whole process of meditation, he feels, may contain a dimension that scientific instruments cannot get at but that cannot be ignored. It's really a study of consciousness that he's doing. With his instruments he can tell that a person is concentrating very deeply—this he could say. But whether a person is concentrating on good or evil, this he couldn't say. But he's prepared to admit that there may be some other discipline that could say something about that. So I believe that the point where science and religion are coming nearest each other is in this whole new science of consciousness, this new science of man and human potential. I remember how shocked I was when I first heard the Buddhists speak of a samadhi of pure evil. In other words, you can get into this deep level of awareness, but it can be either love or hatred that's in you. The development of potential is one thing, but how that potential is used is quite another thing. So I believe that theology now has an opportunity to dialogue with science in a new interdisciplinary way.

Q: Krishnamurti seems to take a dim view of traditional meditation, that it is just sitting and repeating mantras. He seems to think it becomes a mechanical exercise and that a person becomes dependent upon it. He seems to feel it's one's behavior that counts, one's way of life.

JOHNSTON: It's true, it can become a mechanical thing; and in the gospels Christ says that also: "Don't keep talking words like the Gentiles. They think that by talking a lot of words they'll be heard. Don't be like that" (Matthew 6: 7–8). In other words, you need faith. And then if you're repeating the thing with faith, only then can you come to enlightenment. So there could be the danger of its becoming a mechanical process, and I would agree that some kind of faith is necessary as well, Buddhist faith, Christian faith, faith in man, faith in the search—for search is also a kind of faith. If you're searching you believe, you hope that something is to be found. Therefore, I say faith—in the broad sense of the word. Now, as to your action being what counts—it's true, but it's a kind of vicious circle. Of course, it's the whole life that counts, as the Zen Buddhists say: Zen is not just sitting morning and evening. Zen is walking, Zen is eating, Zen is sleeping, Zen is life. It's a kind of deeper awareness that penetrates your whole life. But to get to this deeper awareness, meditation is one way and a valuable way. That it's the only way and that the whole human race has to meditate—that is not what I am saying. But I do believe it is one of the ways to this wisdom, this deeper awareness and this activity in wisdom. But there could be another way—for example, the way of love. If a person is totally dedicated to other people, totally forgetful of self, I believe that he will attain enlightenment through self-forgetfulness in love. So I would not say that meditation is a sort of panacea, a way for everyone. Of course, it has its danger. Everything has its danger.

Q: How are we to think about the apparent "exclusion clauses" in the New Testament—for example, the evangelical approach which says that Jesus of Nazareth is the only way and that all others are a deception?

JOHNSTON: You say that New Testament Christianity is very exclusive, but I wonder. Remember where Christ says that he has not found such faith in all Israel? And where he deliberately chose the Samaritan? He was extremely open to people outside the fold, so to speak. I think that was precisely what infuriated the people of the time, that he kept saying "Well, the people outside the fold know more than we do."

Q (same person): I was thinking more in terms of the Christian bookstores or churches that are warning of the deceptions of the Eastern religions, mysticism, and meditation. How do you deal with this problem? And they use those "exclusion clauses" as evidence that all other ways but Christ are wrong.

JOHNSTON: As I've said, the Second Vatican Council was something of a revolution. And we have to say quite honestly that for the last thousand years or so Christianity does have a history of intolerance and lack of understanding toward other religions. Now I don't think you can sweep that away in one year or so. It will take time and that cannot be helped. But on the other hand, to warn people against the dangers, against the difficulties—I think that's a good idea, too.

Because any kind of mysticism at all, whether Christian or Buddhist, is a rather tricky business in many ways. It's easy to go the wrong way. Therefore, a kind of moderate warning to people to be careful is not so bad. The resolution of this whole problem will in any case take time, generations perhaps.

Q: There has always been a great deal of talk in Christian churches about sin. It has been almost like a scare campaign. I have never heard this sort of thing coming from Zen.

JOHNSTON: Let us take sin not as my personal action but as the human condition, what Christians call original sin. There's something comparable to that in Buddhism too—the idea that man is in a rather unfortunate situation, that he's weak, and that the world he lives in is an illusion. You find that in both Buddhism and Paul's Epistle to Romans. The Buddhist question is: how to get out of that? How to get out of the mess man is in? And they answer: through enlightenment man is liberated. The Christian puts man in original sin because of his refusal to love, his abuse of love. And he too needs salvation and can be saved by enlightenment, except that it's an enlightenment of faith, faith in Christ. But perhaps you are saying that there's been a kind of unhealthy sense of guilt instilled in Christians?

Q: ... Yes.

JOHNSTON: To that I can only say it is very unfortunate. . . . These things happen. I'm sorry. Things can always be badly misunderstood in any religion. It always happens. It's part of the sin, part of what human nature is.

Tibetan Buddhism:
The Way of Inward Discovery

Lobsang Phuntsok Lhalungpa

. . .
.

As WE DISCUSS BUDDHISM, one of the major spiritual cultures in the world today, let us consider it as a common heritage of mankind. In order to establish a communication between us, we need to bring about a moment of freedom so that we may be able to give our full attention to what is being said. In our tradition we first remind the audience of the art of listening; it consists of abandoning obstacles and creating favorable circumstances, both environmental and psychological. People are urged to jettison the Three Obstacles to good listening, just as they leave their shoes at the front door of the temple.

The Three Obstacles are described by an analogy with three types of containers: (1) a container placed upside-down cannot receive anything; it suggests a complete lack of interest and attention; (2) one that has a hole suggests partial attention but lack of interest; (3) one that stinks suggests obstructions such as prejudices, expectations of advantage, skepticism, or bad motivation. Besides environmental and circumstantial tranquillity a motivation oriented toward the noble aim of universal emancipation is important, as well as psychological conditions such as open-mindedness.

We will not be disappointed if we do not allow ourselves to be guided by our fantasies. One such fantasy is the expectation of finding a novel way to an "instant enlightenment" or psychic power, either from the ancient teachings or by creating new ones that blend the ancient and the modern knowledge. Amidst confusion and crisis we find ourselves drifting aimlessly, hoping to find a new light along the way. It is quite possible for us to find such a light, a new way toward a lasting basis of happiness, if we have a genuine urge and determination consistent with a purpose and a goal. Opportunities are not lacking; yet overzealousness should not blind us to the need for caution.

Some vital questions were raised in the introductory lecture reflecting the mood and spirit of many serious-minded people. One of the questions was whether the esoteric traditions of ancient times have the power to lead modern man toward a struggle for real consciousness. To me, the real question seems to be whether people will have a strong enough urge to be willing to undergo the rigors of esoteric training, working their way quietly toward a true spiritual awakening, or whether they will ignore training and true experience with the ostensible purpose of adapting esoteric knowledge to the need of modern man.

How will or should modern initiates readjust themselves? Will they or should they conform totally to the traditional mode of living and forms of practices, and separate themselves from the culture of their own society? Or should they equate everything esoteric with modern psychological theories and even reduce the means of self-awakening to a mechanical exercise for the masses, with the intent of enhancing physical rather than spiritual welfare?

Unless prospective initiates are capable of absorbing the real spirit of esotericism and of adapting the esoteric discipline to their circumstances and needs without undermining the true purpose of the spiritual training, it is unlikely that a true esoteric tradition will take deep roots in a free society.

However, the present trend among many people toward a simpler mode of living and toward working for a higher consciousness can be a mere shift in form, unless these inclinations are utilized for a real inward transformation. For the masses of people with different backgrounds and cultures, who cannot escape the pressures of the modern way of life and who are caught up in the real struggle for existence without any deeper purpose, Buddhism, with its diverse approaches, may have something worth while to offer.

Tibetan Buddhism is an integrated version of the teachings of the Buddha, comprising a multiple system collectively known as the Three Vehicles, namely Hinayana, Mahayana, and Vajrayana—the Lesser Vehicle, the Great Vehicle, and the Indestructible Vehicle. It is a conglomeration of the various traditional streams of Buddhism, which flowed into Tibet from neighboring countries such as India, Nepal, Kashmir, and China. These teachings were designed to meet the requirements of various types of individuals and levels of spiritual development.

From the seventh century, when Buddhism was formally intro-

duced into Tibet, the Tibetan people generally underwent a transformation from their martial traits and military pursuits to a peaceful
spiritual dedication. The massive scriptures and literature translated accurately and beautifully from Sanskrit and Chinese, as
well as the literary output by the Tibetans themselves covering a
wide range of subjects, were astonishingly great. So also was the
number of spiritually awakened men and women.

The character of Buddhism can be deduced from the definitive
term in Tibetan *nangpai-cho*—"the way of the inward seeker." Buddhism propounds the theory that the origin of the cycle of existence
(*samsara*) is ignorance of a most fundamental kind, devoid of insight into the true nature of all things and the working of the
natural law (*karma*). And one might say that all our sorrows are
the result of those of our past attitudes and actions that were ignoble and harmful, whereas our happiness is the result of those that
were noble and beneficial. The present state of our mind and action
is an indication of our future. The implication is that our destiny
lies in our own hands. We must work out our liberation once and
for all, because we are blessed with a human life and its qualities,
both manifest and hidden.

The Buddha said in one of his final messages:

> I have shown you the path of liberation.
> Know that it depends upon yourself.

So one does not seek and depend upon external authorities in
shaping one's final destiny, but, as the Buddha also said, "One is
one's own protector."

One may ask, what is liberation all about? It is simply a state of
freedom from delusion and defilement, which may be positively
described as awakened insight into the true nature of man and his
world, mind, and matter. Our fundamental ignorance creates a world
of duality and false reality out of its inner delusion and fantasy.

"*Samsara* and *nirvana* are not a duality," said Master Phakpa Lha.
"Knowledge concerning the innate nature of *samsara* is designated
as *nirvana*." Thus, the distinction between the "cycle of existence"
(*samsara*) and the "state of freedom" (*nirvana*) is explicitly based
on "unawareness" and "awareness." In other words, the difference
between an ignorant person and an enlightened one lies in a state
of mind—which either lacks or possesses "awakened insight." It is
said, "Milk is the original source of butter. One does not get butter

unless one devotes oneself to churning the milk well. Sentient beings are the original source of Buddhas. One does not attain Buddhahood unless one devotes oneself to the meditative process."

What is the true nature of things? If liberation is simply insight into that intrinsic nature, is the human intellect, with its faculties, capable of comprehending it? The true nature of things is popularly known as Buddha-nature. The term *Buddha* may be viewed from an abstract and impersonal standpoint, since it is the universal character of all things—phenomena and noumena. The Buddha only discovered and proclaimed it. Neither he nor, for that matter, any other Buddha was responsible for its existence. There is a saying that the Buddha-nature has never been ennobled by Enlightened Ones or made ignoble by ignorant beings. Consistent with the term "the naturally indwelling character," Buddha-nature is an abstract state of total simplicity, *sunyata*—emptiness.

The true nature of things is *no nature* in an ultimate sense, since all things except *sunyata* and space are composite and conditioned. Whatever is conditioned by cause and effect, by the interrelation between constituent parts and a composite whole, cannot be real. The absence of such reality is the Suchness of Emptiness, the all-encompassing universality—the substratum of all things and therefore the natural source of all potentialities, despite its being befogged temporarily by the inner veil before us. The human intellect in its deluded state does not and cannot comprehend emptiness, let alone realize it, without breaking loose from the powerful spell of delusion and defilement. Discovering Buddha-nature is truly a complete process of discovering man himself, and through this process, discovering the universality of truth.

The real test lies not so much in aspirations and actions, which are from the relative view distinct and formally discriminatory, as in their true intent—that is to say, whether they reinforce the fortress of self-delusion and ego or transform them into enlightened awareness unfolding its noblest sentiment, compassion. All noble endeavors—including intellectual enrichment, religious devotion, moral observance, and spiritual exercise—can become a kind of "refined bondage"; yet seemingly materialistic pursuits can ennoble oneself and may benefit many. I will illustrate this point with an anecdote:

King Prasenajit of Kosala once asked the Buddha, "O blessed Lord, pray enlighten me as to why I have not had a glimpse of Illumination, despite my vast achievement of virtuous deeds." The

Buddha replied, "Honored king, virtuous deeds cannot be measured. Truth will remain beyond the reach of one who holds fast to his image of being virtuous."

This naturally leads us to a related question as to what constitutes a complete teaching—one that touches all sides of human nature. One cannot deal with Buddhism comprehensively in a brief moment. Its presentation in a condensed or simplified form will not give a clear picture or do justice to Buddhism. Therefore, I will deal only with some of the more vital aspects.

In its own way, Buddhism includes not only all sides of human nature but also all sentient beings and the phenomenal world within the cosmic cycle of existence. With penetrating insight, it starts from a deep concern with sorrows and the cause of the sorrows of all sentient beings in the immeasurable universe full of worlds, and it offers possible solutions in all the diverse forms that man can explore. It inculcates in him a sense of moral discrimination that may be defined as a universal empathy, reinforced by self-discipline and self-transformation. It declares that distinctions among people based on their physical characteristics, family background, social standing, and so forth, are nothing but manifestations of ignorance and prejudice. It seeks to open in man eyes of knowledge, wisdom, and enlightenment—eyes capable of distinguishing actuality from appearance, penetrating the frontier of knowledge, and seeing clearly how man confuses his illusory inner image with "absolute reality," even though both illusion and reality are subjective formulations. It proclaims that all sentient beings will ultimately achieve liberation by discovering the hidden light, the Buddha-nature. It shows the whole process of breaking man's inner barriers, which are the source of distortion and disquiet, and of bringing out natural qualities by harnessing physical and mental energies as beneficial media for gaining deeper experience and illumination.

Buddhism, then, is a way of life, a consummate psychotherapy, a science of mind, a means of exploring the mysteries and the marvels of man, a code of ethics based on the cultivation of a higher sense of purpose, a humanism of a high order, a profound metaphysics, a rational approach with its own form of critical investigation, a proven way of exploring man's intellectual and emotional resources, a pacifier of psychophysical disquiet, an all-comprehending view gained through meditation and mental training. Its esoteric way seeks to transform man completely by special methods of harnessing all that is brutal and base in him, including all his sensory and sensual experiences, to the service of higher ends. This process is described as turning poison into nectar.

In the integrated system of Buddhism there exist two distinct lines of approach based on particular patterns of response in individuals. They are the rapid way and the gradual way. The rapid way is for individuals who display an unusual urge for spiritual insight, or for those who respond to a great master with a profound understanding and devotion. They may receive any aspect of the higher teachings—selective initiation and instruction, followed by secret oral transmissions in proportion to their progress of understanding and awakening—or any teaching their master sees fit to impart. They may even be subjected to tests by their master, such as being assigned tasks that demand much tenacity, tolerance, and trust—without obvious relationship to their expectation.

The gradual way is a path to train aspirants through stages. As a comprehensive theory and method integrating diverse approaches considered necessary for those seeking complete self-training, it sets out to meet the needs of individuals who have urges and aspirations, courage and capability, in varying depth and diversity. In this exhaustive practice, spiritual aspirants are classified according to three levels: elementary, intermediate, and advanced. Each level represents types of human being; is based on their specific attitudes, aspirations, and abilities; and corresponds to one of three stages of training. Individuals on lower levels of spiritual development must necessarily endeavor to reach the advanced levels. Those who already show discernible signs of having reached an advanced level must start from the elementary stage in order to build a stable foundation of understanding and self-cultivation.

Through this terrain of comprehensive training flow multiple streams, representing different forms of the Buddha's teaching and various lines of approach that come to us directly from the great Master. From the standpoint of historical tradition, there are two major sources of these teachings: the Primary and the Great Vehicles. The Primary Vehicle is now represented by the forms of Buddhism prevalent in Burma, Thailand, Ceylon, and other countries, while the Great Vehicle is practiced in Japan, Nepal, Bhutan, and Sikkim, as well as among overseas Chinese and Tibetans. Self-liberation is the aim of the Primary Vehicle, whereas universal liberation is the aim of the Great Vehicle.

A spiritual way must be comprehensive so as to deal with all sides of the human structure. Buddhism does so not merely by detecting man's problems but also by penetrating more deeply into their causes and offering diverse but definite means to overcome these very problems and to achieve liberation.

In order to undergo the complete training as a lay person, one must have the understanding necessary to apply oneself to the required practice. The doctrinal theory consists of three phases—namely, (1) the foundation, (2) the path, and (3) the goal.

The theory of the foundation reveals the causes of the cycle of existence, man's happiness and sorrows, his spiritual potentiality, and the innate character of human awareness as Buddha-nature. The potentialities that manifest themselves in man are different in form and degree; in some they are manifested as an innate longing for the ennoblement of one's attitude and the elevation of one's consciousness and action, in others as a deep urge for a highly detached consciousness, and in yet others as a universal compassion.

The path is the application of the theory in one's daily life, appropriate to each stage of training and its progressive realization. In practical terms, an aspirant endeavors to gain perfect viewpoints concerning the nature of himself and his environment, both in appearance and in actuality. But perfect viewpoints do not come about by the mere exercise of human intellect; they are the natural outcome of wisdom—that is to say, "awakened insight" capable of comprehending all facets of truth. Through wisdom one can see ignorance as the cause of delusion, which, in turn, is the source of deceptive discrimination and confused speculation, as well as of prejudice and self-clinging. Thus, through ignorance one confuses what is false and illusory with what is true and actual. One confuses material pursuits with the true purpose of life, transitoriness with permanence, the conditioned with the unconditioned, unity of perception with duality, the relative aspect with the ultimate aspect, "emptiness of reality" with nothingness, and so on.

It is said that the path of wisdom is meant for those who have hardly any dust on their eyes, as we say in Tibet, whereas the path of faith is for those who, to use a Christian phrase, see through a glass darkly. Yet one who develops wisdom often falls prey to his own ego, so he is equally in need of faith as a counterweight to pride and conceit, even if for no other reason. Faith inspires the faithful, sustains their spirit and courage, engenders humility and

earnestness, helps to check the ego, and inculcates a deep appreciation of those human qualities whose ultimate embodiments one
perceives in the Enlightened Ones. And it is faith and wisdom that
solidify conviction in the deeper knowledge that one continues to
gain. Even as aspirants are urged toward the need to develop faith,
they are made aware of its intrinsic limits. Faith is useless unless it
leads to wisdom.

In our tradition spiritual training without a great master is of no
real value. The choice of a personal teacher is as important as the
spiritual pursuit itself. For the training to be fruitful, one must
choose a teacher who is not only learned and competent but also
very compassionate and highly awakened. It is true that any smooth
and successful practice depends as much on one's own understanding
and endeavor as on the progressive transmission of the secret oral
teachings and the frank discussion with and experienced guidance of
the teacher. Yet in the ultimate analysis it is the aspirant himself
who has to apply the scheme of training, formulated according to
his requirements, and he himself must work out his goal of liberation.

Buddhism recognizes that every man is capable of discovering the
truth through his own efforts. Sakyamuni Buddha said:

> Buddhas do not wash away the effects of defilements,
> Nor do they remove the sorrows of sentient beings,
> Nor do they even transfer their realization to others,
> But by showing "the truth of all nature,"
> They proclaim deliverance.

A beginning is made by hearing discourses from one's teacher, and
the understanding thus gained may be strengthened by reading appropriate texts and by clearing up doubts through further discussions
and personal reflection. In this way one corroborates what one understands about oneself and one's world from personal observation,
both inward and outward. Furthermore, one learns how to examine
critically and systematically whatever is experienced and observed.

Next, concentrative meditation helps to calm mental agitation and
disquiet, bringing in its wake psychophysical harmony, equanimity,
and bliss, so that any kind of deeper meditation, where the trance
state alternates with the analytical, becomes truly enlightening. Thus,
one may be able to penetrate beyond the known into the unknown,
and to explore the Ultimate Nature behind deceptive forms and
concepts. True discernment of the intrinsic nature of illusory ap-

pearance can and will bring about an "illuminating" awakening to the unity of all things in an ultimate sense, an awakening to the interdependence of appearance and the emptiness of reality.

The deep insight described earlier requires preparation. The elementary training is the foundation of the succeeding ones. The purpose here is limited to developing the human potentialities of normal man. The pupil should recognize his own human existence and consider it as the basis of opportunities for a noble pursuit, provided he is of sound body and intelligent mind. He should be capable of developing a humane attitude and an urge to harmonize his material and spiritual pursuits. Mindful of the natural consequences of unwholesome and harmful thoughts and actions, he should endeavor throughout his meditation and his daily actions to be vigilant and to control any gross passions such as extreme selfishness, greed, jealousy, pride, and hatred. His conduct and all manner of speech must be nonviolent, not merely in an absence of violence and abuse but also as a positive expression of kindness and social concern.

The objects of observation and meditation at this stage are the theory of cause and effect, with its moral implications, and the transitory aspect of all things. Understanding these—the law of nature (*karma*) and the fleeting changes of every moment—will enable man to pursue his spiritual ideals here and now. He should concern himself with the "excellence of each moment."

Normally we are conscious of the larger and more obvious aspects of impermanence, such as changes in the weather, the alternation of seasons, or the process of aging, but the more subtle changes that take place from moment to moment escape our attention—perhaps because people everywhere feel it a waste of time to observe and be aware of the immense changes that take place within us, outside us, around us, everywhere and all the time. This seems to be an example of how we, as civilized human beings, avoid simple ways of glimpsing the truth that lies constantly before our eyes. Truth does not hide itself beneath the surface. Our delusion has driven it there. Since our minds have been conditioned, we compartmentalize truth and limit its scope, and so we find it hard to believe in the existence of simple ways to discover facets of truth. We cannot find truth in an ultimate sense until we manage to break the shackles of our prejudices and conditionings. Yet we are capable of gaining a moment of freedom, if we really care, just by observing and rationally examining the transitoriness of things.

Momentary change is an irrefutable and universal fact of nature. The evidence of it is available in ample measure. Birth and death are not widely divided events. All composite things are subject to momentary change. A moment of birth is followed by its death. Every moment we are born and every consecutive moment we are dying, not only physically but mentally as well. Like our physical body, our mental consciousness is a flux of events. Considering the changing nature of things in the universe and the variable pattern of human relationships, an aspirant should harmonize his own attitudes toward people and overcome his prejudice and his dislike of certain things and people.

We human beings complicate our own lives. We impose our willful assumptions and expectations on the natural scheme of things, imagining life to be what we desire and crave. We expect only desirable and pleasurable things to happen. We even expect changes to take place in a manner that is acceptable to us.

Nevertheless, with all its defects and limitations, fragility and frailty, man's body and mind, technically called the "aggregate of psychophysical elements," is the best vehicle capable of transporting us, in this very life, across the sea of misery and dissatisfaction into a realm of beauty, peace, and happiness, if only we are seriously interested in using our potentialities, our hidden treasure, to the utmost.

It is possible that a pragmatic person may easily see the momentary transitoriness of existence while lacking the understanding, either inborn or acquired, to go deeper. What if he sees only a hollowness of life, devoid of any real stability, security, or basis of true happiness in such a swirling storm of changes? Disillusionment and frustration are his lot. He finds himself confused and lost. What has happened to him is not necessarily unusual or bad. The simple discovery of the way things are has shattered his image of life, which had no relationship with actuality. It is the beginning of the end of his delusion. A sensible person would treat this as a realistic basis of a new attitude toward life and would endeavor to act in a way truly beneficial for himself and his fellow men.

The purpose of observing the changing nature of things is to make an aspirant conscious of all aspects of life: good, bad, and neutral. Would it not be a tragic defeat for a hero to engage his opponent in battle without first knowing his strength and weakness, his weapons and strategy? So we must acquaint ourselves with life's illusions and realities if our battle of life is to be worth while.

The training at the intermediate stage helps an aspirant to discover *nonselfhood*, the nature of mind, through the cultivation of nonattachment toward all sensory objects and experiences; of an aversion to the transient and sorrowful state of the existential cycle; of a strong urge for personal liberation and also of a devotion toward a higher transformation of his consciousness, expressed in the qualities of good will and compassion conjoined with nonviolent conduct. The concept of nonviolence at this level assumes such strong significance that a devotee is required to abstain from violence even at the cost of his own life.

Observation commensurate with the various stages of training becomes more and more exhaustive as one advances to higher and higher stages of training and awakening. An observer in the intermediate stage sees how absurd it is for an aspirant to wish to remain continuously in the realm of *samsara.* One's body and mind—the aggregate of psychophysical elements—are often subject to the pain of injury and anguish; even the pleasures one experiences are so fleeting and changeable that they soon wear out the senses, leaving one dissatisfied. Moreover, a strong and healthy body is in fact so fragile that the slightest increase in heat or cold causes the greatest torment. The human mind, with all its conditioning, is even more frail. It is hurt by many things. With its self-craving, its attachment and intolerance, and all its other blemishes, it is constantly agitated. The root cause of this mental disquiet is a distorted view of life, stemming from one's delusion and desire. Attachment to sensory gratification and egoistic craving is not only deceptive but also damaging to one's true peace. The significant difference between those who are prepared through conscious effort in their training and those who have a distorted view of life lies in the fact that the latter will aggravate their situation, while the former will open their minds to true insight.

Checking attachment is often difficult even for a well-trained spiritual person, unless he is relentlessly vigilant. Once a mad saint, Kunle, quietly removed a precious garment and some jewelry that were hidden away in a monastic treasury and then proceeded to climb the mountain behind the monastery. Great consternation arose. The abbot and a host of functionaries rushed to the terrace of the monastery to see what the mad saint was doing. Suddenly he came rolling down the mountainside like a log, wearing the precious garment and jewelry. Everybody was in great fear that these treasures might be destroyed and that the mad saint would be killed. But he immediately sprang up and went to the abbot, who was distraught with worry. Delivering everything intact, the mad saint told the abbot he wanted to destroy the abbot's attachment to these precious things. The abbot thereupon admitted his great fault.

By the overcoming of attachments, peace is more easily achieved in this life. The search for this peace lies in working for one's liberation from all existential bondage. Bondage means one's ignorance of truth, one's deluded vision, the craving for selfhood, deceptive discrimination, greed and hatred, and so on. Life's positive aspects are its purity and a peace endowed with awakened insight. Thus, this simple liberation is called *nirvana*—a state beyond sorrow.

One may attain *nirvana* in this very life by acquiring insight into the causes of both misery and happiness, seeking in the wake of such insight the elimination of self-delusion and defilements and the expansion of a deeper vision ennobling one's consciousness. In order to determine the true nature of mind and matter one should examine one's notion of selfhood—expressed as "I" and "mine"—and the definition of this concept in all its variety. Here one dwells upon one's understanding of the concept of nonselfhood; one rejects the notion of an independent self, eternal and substantive, on one hand, and one rejects nihilism on the other. Such an examination will lead one to the understanding of the true nature of man himself.

In order to penetrate into this true nature one examines the two aspects of truth that deal with appearance and reality. One of the early Buddhist schools, belonging to the Hinayana tradition, defines relative truth as the empirical knowledge of the conditioned and ultimate truth as the knowledge of the real. Relative truth is that which normally appears real to us but cannot stand close scrutiny in terms of ultimate reality. The ultimate truth can be appreciated by means of the concept of objective reality. Hinayana tradition teaches that matter is reducible to its ultimate condition of subatomic particles. Mind, as the continual flux of consciousness, is in its turn reducible to its infinitesimal moments of awareness. Hence, consciousness is conditioned by many factors. There is only becoming, and thus our notion of selfhood as substantive and eternal is an obstacle to the realization of truth.

A well-coordinated and -harmonized practice visualizes two primary areas of life as spiritually creative and beneficial: contemplative life and active life. In contemplative practice one's energy and endeavor are all directed toward achieving quietude and mental tranquillity through one-pointed concentration, and a penetrating analytical insight in a meditation which culminates in a trance equilibrium. It is here that one enters deeply into awareness of the true nature of mind. The Middle Path of the Buddha applied to meditation rejects the total suppression of all perceptive experiences and discursive thoughts, for such a diversionary course is likely to prevent the meditator from gaining intuitive insight. Nevertheless, one who ignores one-pointed meditation simply to pursue intellectual inquiry, without knowing how to proceed or what to do at a given stage, is sure to create confusion and disharmony within himself. Throughout one's training the right attitude is of primary importance. The importance of attitude may be illustrated here.

A great Lama by the name of Ben Gungyel was expecting some visitors, so he had his shrine redecorated and set up beautifully with lamps, incense, and other such offerings. Then, suddenly and swiftly, he changed his mind and threw a handful of dust at the shrine. His disciples were astounded by this act, which was tantamount to sacrilege. The Lama explained to them that his offerings were stained with impurity as a result of hypocrisy, since they were put up to impress his visitors. Having heard about the incident, another great Lama told his audience that the handful of dust thrown at the shrine was the best offering anyone had ever made.

So far we have been examining certain aspects of the early training in Hinayana tradition. Mahayana Buddhism emphasizes more pointedly the question of universal perspective. Judging from such a universal perspective, a man of great sensitivity or humanistic fervor may be well advised to treat any aspiration toward personal liberation as tantamount to diminishing his true character. Unless he comes to the realization of *universal liberation*, which demands great sacrifices, selfless dedication, an indomitable spirit, and a constant striving, his great potentiality has been wasted.

Consistent with the Bodhisattva[1] vow, which he takes before his chosen master, to work relentlessly toward that goal, the aspirant is required to concentrate on gaining understanding of the Mahayana teachings, the moral and metaphysical doctrines, with the aim of

---

[1] Bodhisattva: one who is on the way to attaining Buddhahood and who vows not to enter nirvana until all sentient beings are liberated from bondage and illusion.—Eds.

creating a faultless view of things. There are two aspects of the great vow: the first is conventional and the second absolute. The conventional aspect concerns itself with the development of infinite compassion and love, the absolute aspect with the development of profound wisdom. This great twofold vow can be carried out in two stages: aspiration and application. The stage of aspiration is for human beings who are striving to reach an awakened condition. They do so by practicing the path known as *skill in means* and through discerning wisdom. "Skill in means" refers to the methods conceived and consummated in one's practice. It is in essence the development of a great compassion. With the light of true knowledge one may be able to clear the darkness of ignorance and the delusion of duality. Wisdom is an understanding of knowledge and an insight into the diverse facets of truth at all levels of one's endeavor and enlightenment.

The method known as skill in means encompasses all aspects of attitude and action born out of an ever-expanding compassion and love. Wisdom and compassion cannot be separated in the actual functioning of man's life. Wisdom is indispensable in achieving personal liberation, for wisdom alone in an ultimate sense is capable of dismantling human bondage, such as the deception of ignorance and "clinging-to-selfhood" in all things, whereas compassion is indispensable in achieving supreme enlightenment. Yet compassion itself is incapable of destroying the root of delusion. Without the ultimate vision of wisdom, compassion on its own cannot achieve the strength to carry out its functions with regard to both unlimited duration of time and magnitude of scope. Hence compassion and wisdom are interdependent. The two principles are the quintessence of Mahayana tradition and the source of ultimate vision, consummated action, and unfolding creativity.

Skill in means, I repeat, encompasses all aspects of attitudes and actions. In practical life an aspirant endeavors to fulfill his great vow by applying the two principles. Besides the overriding principle of wisdom-gone-beyond, the path of skill in means is fivefold as applied to the diverse aspects and stages of an aspirant's life. Its applications are:

(1) generosity-gone-beyond;   (4) striving-gone-beyond;
(2) morality-gone-beyond;   (5) contemplation-gone-beyond.
(3) patience-gone-beyond;

The following analogy may give you a mental picture of the two stages of training in the path of the Bodhisattva.

A man of compassion has resolved to dedicate himself to the noble cause of delivering to a beautiful land a mass of people who are languishing in a wild country. He prepares himself first by seeking knowledge concerning the trackless path—its obstacles and hazards and how to overcome them—as well as the conditions in the wonderful land. Meanwhile, he works hard to remedy his own problems, such as weakness and sickness, and to gain physical strength and stamina, mental stability and sensitivity. He then undertakes the venture and reaches his destination. This stage represents the aspiration and endeavor of a potential Bodhisattva, pragmatic and experimental in nature. The compassionate man then returns to his fellow beings and works for their deliverance. This return represents the stage of enlightened action transcending the pragmatic level of the unenlightened.

To continue the analogy for the six principles of gone-beyond: the mental resolution of the man represents the Bodhisattva's great vow; his nonattachment represents generosity-gone-beyond; his earnest abstention from all harmful thoughts and deeds and his application to beneficial ones represent morality-gone-beyond; his fortitude and forbearance in enduring hardships represent patience-gone-beyond; his relentless endeavor represents striving-gone-beyond; his one-pointed devotion to the cause represents contemplation-gone-beyond; and finally there is his unmatched vision, which represents wisdom-gone-beyond.

This is further illustrated by an excerpt from the *Songs of Milarepa*:

> Beyond the elimination of the grasping of ego
>   There is no generosity of giving apart;
> Beyond the elimination of hypocrisy
>   There is no morality apart;
> Beyond the fearlessness of truth
>   There is no patience apart;
> Beyond the constant application
>   There is no striving apart;
> Beyond the remaining in tranquillity
>   There is no concentration apart;
> Beyond awakening to ultimate truth
>   There is no insight apart;
> Beyond the application to the noble Path
>   There is no skill in means apart. . . .
> Beyond realizing the errors of defilements
>   There is no awareness apart.

Thus, Buddhist practices are designed to help man discover himself fully, so that he may be able to see for himself the shackles of his own bondage, to adopt a truly humane attitude to life, and to transform himself psychologically under the enlightened inspiration of an ultimate vision born out of wisdom.

The right view of life is the effect of developing discerning wisdom. It is an attitude and also a knowledge. Through wisdom one observes oneself and one's world. It is the natural way of looking at things as they truly are and not as they appear to us according to our ideas, concepts, and impressions. By discovering the truth of one thing, one discovers all the rest. Ordinarily, man cognizes some facet of truth through experience and observation with objectivity, yet he has little or no way of directly comprehending truth in an ultimate sense, even though truth is ever present in front of him and within and around him; he is like an ignorant person incapable of identifying a precious jewel that lies in front of him. Can a man expect to get a good view through a telescope when the lens is out of focus with his own optical range, and also when his own eyes are infected?

The doctrinal direction for cultivating right views is that whatever is perceived as "reality" by a deluded mind is mere appearance, having only relative validity. There is no absolute reality in anything thus perceived, yet such perception is the basis of our conceptual functions and imputations. The implication is that the perception lacks any real content, for it is conditioned by cause and effect, that is to say, it is a product of interacting causes and effects. The innate nature of the conditioned is transient and changeable, without even an infinitesimal share of reality. Even supreme enlightenment itself is devoid of any intrinsic reality, because the concept of reality is the product of delusion. The absence of intrinsic reality is the true nature of all things. This is *sunyata*, "emptiness," which should not be confused with nothingness. This knowledge is considered to be all-encompassing, for it concerns the suchness of all nature, which defies any verbal definitions and intellectual predications and evidently is beyond the comprehension of the "deluded intellect."

The key to obtaining either rapid or gradual insight into the depth and diversity of perception is to understand the unity of appearance and actuality—that is, the perception of an image and its emptiness. The essential unity of *samsara* and *nirvana* has to be viewed in the same light.

Observation is indispensable throughout the training toward enlightenment. An aspirant knows that understanding precedes observation, that through observation awareness arises, and that inferential insight follows. One who observes without understanding is like a fool being deceived by a conjuring trick in a magical display. One who observes with understanding is similar to a jeweler who can tell a precious stone from an imitation.

One must know not only how to observe and what to be aware of when observing but also how to appraise the experience and to appreciate it if one is to derive the benefit of gaining deep insight. Even as one observes oneself—for instance, when one is very distressed—the very act itself implies knowledge concerning how to observe, what to be aware of when observing, and when to apply oneself to retrospection. Understanding, observation, and examination are the means to expand wisdom.

Observation is a direct confrontation with the world of appearance. Can our normal observation be as objective as it should be? Buddhism makes a distinction between what is perceived as appearance of a form and our conceptual image of the appearance we perceive. One who can distinguish between what is projected and what actually appears may be considered a good observer. The question, then, is whether such an observer has gained or can gain the necessary understanding concerning the true nature of perception itself. An observer without such understanding is likely to be misled by his own ignorant delusions or to be influenced by intellectual concepts of various kinds. It is hard for an untrained observer to derive any real benefit from his observation. It is often difficult even for one who can distinguish between appearance and actuality and comprehend their interrelationship to gain real insight into the ultimate aspect of an appearance until he achieves enlightenment.

An observer is urged to observe himself inwardly under all circumstances, so as to be aware of his own psychological conditionings. We all know by our own experience our utter failure to observe ourselves in moments of great excitement and distress, particularly when we are overcome with the fire of anger, the intoxication of lust and craving, or the darkness of delusion.

If an observer gains an insight into the innermost aspect of his object through his observation, it must and will leave its imprint upon his conscious mind. He should be able to apprehend, beyond image, notion, or concept, the innate nature of his perception, which is the emptiness of reality. All perceptions and emotions are in themselves devoid of intrinsic reality or attributes, and as such are nothing more than illusions. Illusions are created out of cause and conditions, yet they are capable of evoking response and producing effects. Perception is often clouded with emotion and becomes beneficial only when transmuted into an awakened awareness, a sense of compassion; it is harmful if influenced by attachment, anger, and so on. An awareness of perception, if undisturbed, can cause one to reach a trance state which for that moment is free of all influences. One will even experience a novel sensation of tranquillity and bliss, which is the natural product of psychophysical equilibrium, and as such should not be confused with any real progress or achievement. Incidentally, there seems to be a tendency to glorify visionary experiences as a true measure of spiritual awakening; however, they are in most cases hallucinations or projections of overstimulated emotions.

The great master Tsong-kha-pa says:

Know that all things, internal and external, appearing like magical displays, dreams, and the moon's reflection in placid water, are without any substantive reality. May I be blessed with the consummated meditation of illusion!

Samsara and *nirvana* are without any reality, even to the level of subatomic particles. Cause and effect, being interdependent and interrelated, are undeceiving. May I be blessed with the realization of the two, which are noncontradictory and mutually complementary!

To sum up the training during these three stages: aspirants should examine themselves regarding their achievements and failures. A simple test of true achievement at the elementary stage lies, first, in whether his poignant prejudice, such as a deep attachment to his family and friends on one hand or dislike and hatred for his foes on the other, has been harnessed into a harmonious attitude; and, second, whether he has achieved a greater consciousness of the inevitability and efficacy of the karmic law.

Similarly, the test in the case of those in the intermediate stage lies, first, in whether an aspirant has freed himself from passions and attachments, and, second, in whether he is still overcome with the ways of ignorance—namely, being easily pleased by pleasure, praise, gain, or fame, or aggrieved by their opposites.

In the case of those in the advanced stage, the test lies in whether they have compassion even for their enemies and for those to whom they are indifferent, sympathizing with them for having fallen victim to their own egoism and delusions, their desires and hatreds.

Finally, an aspirant is urged to carry out all his practices, both meditation and action, as well as the diverse functions of life, with an alertness to the manifestations of self-delusion and with a mindfulness of the three realms of excellence. The first of these, which is called the excellence at the beginning, requires him to examine his attitude and motivation at the beginning of each meditation and action, at the same time renewing his great vow. The second, the excellence in the middle, requires him to be aware, during practice, of nonsubstantiality and nonselfhood, known as "emptiness." And the third, the excellence at the end, requires him to dwell, free from any concept of clinging to the reality of subject, object, and action, in a state of complete awareness.

Returning from the state of trance awareness, one reactivates the sentiment of great compassion for all sentient beings. One is urged to contemplate the four boundless attitudes: the wish (1) that all sentient beings, who are one's fathers and mothers,[1] be in peace and the cause of peace; (2) that they be free from sorrow and the source of sorrow; (3) that they never be separated from peace, unbroken by sorrow; and (4) that they be in a state of equanimity, free from attachment and aversion.

The simplest message of Mahayana Buddhism, therefore, is, that if one is prepared to transform self-love into universal love, he has qualified himself as a Bodhisattva, worthy of esoteric initiation and secret oral transmission in the original sense of the term.

I will close with a quotation from the great teacher Shantideva: "All sorrows of existence come from self-love; all happiness in life comes from love of others." If one is true to the ideal of self-discovery and self-transformation, one does not and cannot allow spiritual achievements to become golden fetters.

QUESTIONS AND ANSWERS

Q: *I've been told that it's a flaw in listening to wish for gain. But I do not understand how to listen with interest but not for gain. Could you explain that to me?*

[1] I.e., intimately connected to oneself in the beginningless cycle of cause and effect (*samsara*).—Ed.

LHALUNGPA: *It depends on what you expect by listening to something. If it is simple desire to know the way of solving some of the important problems that you face in life, then it is possible to listen with simple attention without expectation of gain. If we are to achieve true peace inwardly we should overcome obstacles, particularly those originating from our mind, such as expectation of gain or fear of loss. There is no need to anticipate peace, for it is the innate nature of our inmost consciousness. We can simply activate it through immediate action. Similarly, when a listener becomes listening itself, the result is an extraordinary observation, full of awareness. Our attitude as motive force behind such action also has to be detached from selfishness.*

Q: Buddhism asks us to have an attitude of compassion and nonviolence. Yet these ideas are awfully alien to what our culture does and teaches. What is the Buddhist answer to someone who can start out a day saying "Today I will try not to be violent" but who then finds that he is violent at every turn, even in his approach to nonviolence?

LHALUNGPA: *Nonviolence is a primary principle in Buddhist life. It must be practiced even in the midst of action, speech, and relationships with people. But unless there is a personal willingness or urge to become nonviolent, the precept is absolutely useless. A simple precept does not make a man nonviolent. It is not difficult for one who tries single-mindedly to free himself from the fire of his anger or hatred. With a detached attitude and direct observation one seeks to expose the very root of his violence—the injured self that is under the momentary spell of self-attachment and deceptive discrimination. A moment of violence can be a golden opportunity for a seeker to be transformed into compassion and vision, like producing nectar out of poison.*

Q: Living as we do in a state of duality—samsara—isn't it true that we need to recognize our violence while at the same time understanding the need for nonviolence? Is knowledge of violence nonviolent?

LHALUNGPA: *Oh, yes. Without the knowledge of violence, including its limitations, harmful effects, and its innate nature, one cannot become nonviolent.*

The Samkhya of India:
A Conscious Struggle toward Reality

Lizelle Reymond

. . .

.

I WISH TO SPEAK to you not only from "book knowledge" but also from my experiences in India in order to explore what the Samkhya tradition offers in answer to our present need.

I shall purposely not rely on any of those Sanskrit words that are often said to be necessary for conveying the different stages of spiritual life, and that are also said to be untranslatable into English. My master and several other masters I have met are of the opinion that anything of value expressed in Sanskrit can be translated, since reality is the same everywhere. But we people of the West, with our sense of efficiency, forget that an Eastern man may consecrate a lifetime to obtain what we expect to possess after only a few weeks of serious study. Though we have created machines that can obtain results quickly and effectively, we have to learn that the inner development of man is itself extremely slow. Because of our nature and the laws governing it, we are really as slow as a bullock cart to reach any inner goal.

The Samkhya of which I shall speak is Asia's most ancient form of psychologically based nonreligious thought. At the same time it is a deeply spiritual teaching. The central practical question posed by this Samkhya is how, in reality, one can live in accordance with the cosmic laws, laws not dictated by man.

I shall not speak to you of the philosophical Samkhya, which is the only one known and discussed in the West, and which is a profoundly negative philosophy, but of the Samkhya that is a mystical system enshrined in the Vedas and the Upanishads and that gives many clues as to how to live within onself. Is it possible to connect the concepts of this ancient tradition with modern living as we stumble along in life, constantly subjected to powerful external influences?

Between the teachings of this tradition and modern life, there is an immense zone in which man is and has always been, at the very root of himself, a rebel. This basic instinct of rebellion is that in us which perceives a liberty to which we aspire, while, at the same time, feeling the weight of the heavy walls that imprison us and from which we cannot escape except by our own efforts.

It is toward this rebel within us that I would like us to direct our attention, since in the actual realities of life as we now experience it, whether in Asia, Europe, or the United States, we are all, more or less, rebels. We are therefore faced with the need to discover a completely new manner of thinking: first, to learn how to use the concepts of past civilizations right in the very heart of our present life; and, second, to know how to use the force of life hidden in us for the process of our own evolution.

Samkhya proceeds from two essential concepts that can form the rational basis of our thinking: (1) that of the Spirit (*Purusha*), and (2) that of the Manifestation (*Prakriti*), which is essentially mechanical, as are all the cosmic laws that govern us. Through this description, we are projected into the very heart of Great Nature, without religion, without ritual, without dogma. It is said that all aspects of life can be explained from the point of view of Samkhya, since it uses a psychological language that, by direct experience, can be understood by each one of us.

Tradition tells us that this very practical philosophy was brought to earth in the remote past by the sage Kapila. The first person to be benefited was a woman, Devahuti, identified with the symbol of the earth. She was so pure that she lived completely naked in Great Nature. Having realized knowledge to its ultimate limits, she transformed herself voluntarily at the moment of dying into an inexhaustible river to water the earth, so that thousands of beings could quench their thirst for knowledge in her.

This allegory signifies that Samkhya, which springs directly from the Vedas, contains the secret power that has nourished both the Aryans, in the elaboration of their rules honoring the hundred thousand gods and goddesses of Hinduism, and the rebels, who ran away from the Aryans to live their own lives. These latter are known through a common name: the Vratyas.

In order to be recognized, these rebels wear an ample garment of wool, white, black, or yellow: others, like the Shivaites, live with their naked bodies covered with ashes; others go along singing like the Bauls, known as "god-mad." All these rebels live with a total sense of freedom, without any denomination. And they all claim Samkhya as their origin. The elements of Samkhya, precisely because they are spiritual without being religious, enable one to connect the things from beyond with the things of the world. These elements are without artifice, proceeding by deduction from a perfect superior law which is that of life itself.

As soon as this process is recognized, one enters into a living *spiritual existentialism,* in which new relationships are established between the different centers of the human being: the higher intelligence next to the natural intelligence, the soul and the ego, with their own particular sensitivities and powers of perception. This new way of thinking and living is really a descent from the spirit into matter. The seeker is touched in his inner being.

From this moment, the seeker enters voluntarily into a discipline going toward an ascending consciousness, discovering, step by step, an equilibrium never glimpsed before, or finding again an equilibrium lost in the difficult circumstances that have troubled him. Even if, in the course of this research, the seeker rigorously tries to banish imagination and emotions to the point of what may seem to be a frightening dryness, he is simultaneously nourished by a love from a power which is that of life itself, without any sentimental roots in human love. The science of Samkhya, based on logic and mathematics relative to cosmic laws, can make a saint of a man who has no more faith, either in God or in himself.

But what does the seeker need? He needs an authentic master who shows him the way, who holds him by his hand until he is capable, by himself, of responding to life. It is most difficult to discover this master. A seeker who desires to break away from his habitual ways of ordinary life knows this very well. He has heard and read about it. He knows many things about the "spiritual ways," particularly that they can be dangerous. The traditional image is that the pathway is narrow as a razor's edge. In our modern life, where nothing traditional is recognized, neither family nor religion, the seeker seeks a master who is a *superman* of direct experience.

If my eyes had been opened during the years 1930 to 1935 in Europe, I might have met G. I. Gurdjieff. Gurdjieff was a pioneer who revealed to Western man a way of searching, bare of any artifice, focused on the essential principles of creation in the universe and in man. But it was necessary for me, after twenty years of continuous work in translating the basic texts of Shri Ramakrishna,

Swami Vivekananda, Shri Aurobindo, and others, to go alone into the Himalayas. I had a desire similar to that of thousands of young people today who travel to the East seeking a new dimension, a new thought, to formulate the real question: "Who am I? Who can help me? What will give a direction to my life, enlarge my level of consciousness, harmonize my life with that of the universe that surrounds me?"

But this master one seeks is not seated in the heart of an ashram surrounded by disciples, or in an established community. One of his principal traits is his ability to conceal himself. He is *par excellence* one whom one seeks for a long time and whom one succeeds in finding only with difficulty. His approach is difficult. To discover him, the seeker must already be engaged in a spiritual search; otherwise he will not recognize the master, who may be living in the mob of a bazaar. For the master is without any special appearance, often poor and self-effacing. If one questions him, he may say he knows nothing, that he has nothing to teach and nothing to give. He is often taken for a "simpleton," an illiterate to whom one would willingly give charity.

The seeker is baffled by this total self-effacement, which is unexpected. He loses his bearing. This self-effacement is in fact the counterpart of the assiduity, curiosity, and eagerness of the seeker. In this connection, I shall never forget my first meeting with Shri Anirvan, the master of Samkhya who watched over me for five years while I was in his close circle. I had made a four-day march into the wild forest with a caravan to reach the village where he was living alone writing a commentary on the Vedas. Seated on the floor, we remained for more than an hour, his eyes looking into mine, without a word being spoken. During this terrible ordeal, all my past life was liquified. He then asked, "How much time do you wish to devote to work with me?" I heard myself responding, "As long as you think necessary."

I had found the master who was to take me in hand and then one day send me back to my country. Here was the master who was to respond by negation to all that arose within me. This was to become an essential part of his teaching. Six months later, after having organized my personal affairs in Calcutta, I rejoined him in his remote village in the Himalayas to start work under his guidance. The apparent indifference with which he always treated me was allied to a great caring, forming part of the strategy of Samkhya to create

between us an indestructible trust quite outside of any personal relationship.

Thus, I found myself at work with a small number of followers
that he had gathered together. One cannot speak of disciples, because this implies a submission to the master, which was never the
case for any of us. Each one of us lived in his own way, facing his
own question and the anguish of his own life, which had motivated
him toward a profound personal search.

Before speaking of the practical concepts of Samkhya, it is necessary to indicate on what the follower of Samkhya must lean, since
he has neither submission nor veneration nor adoration to help him,
as he does in all religious disciplines. He is supported only by his
attitude of being, with a conscious effort to understand how to
enlarge his level of consciousness. He knows that the demands of
Samkhya will bring his inner being back to what is most fundamental and primitive in him. He knows also that the aim is to
establish, little by little, a conscious relationship between himself
and others as well as between himself and the entire cosmos. To
establish his search, he uses everything that he has discovered and
experienced—that is, all the events of his life—without passing
judgment on any of them. The self-effacement of the master before
every dogmatic principle becomes the seeker's model.

Contrary to psychoanalytic methods, the follower of Samkhya is led
step by step never to allow his thoughts to take the road backward,
but rather to find the relationship that exists between the universe
that he knows and the unknown universe that surrounds him. He
learns to feel himself as being one of the links of an absolute whole.
He has neither prayer nor demand. His attitude is a living question
facing the "perfect law of life" that unfolds. He comes to know that
it is in meeting obstacles that the inner being makes the necessary
effort to reach a level of consciousness far more vast. To hold himself there becomes the aim, which requires an attentive vigilance,
such that the events of his life, both past and constantly arising, do
not hide the vision of the whole. It is necessary to have much
patience and perseverance. Such a life is truly a life of prayer. The
master himself extends his hand to his pupil and supports him. At
the same time, he remains mute no matter what is brought to him;
otherwise the search would stop. The master never says what there
is to be done. The experience of the very moment is what matters.
Each one of us had his own field of personal experimentation.

For my part, while in the Himalayas with Shri Anirvan, I was continuing to write the life of a saint, with the aim of delving into the unfolding of his revelation. For some years, I had lived identified with my subject, eager to know, seeking information; I had interviewed many people who had known this saint. The master appreciated my ardor and showed it by providing me with some valuable information. He encouraged me, but at the same time he left me to flounder. That stage was to last several months until something resulted, something I had not anticipated, an upsetting of values—a veritable uprooting. The master remained mute. It was for me to discover that the spiritual element can be neither seized nor analyzed nor understood apart from its physical support. For the first time, I was faced with the discipline of Samkhya, a discipline which affirms that everything is reality.

Everything is reality down to the lowest mechanical manifestation. But there is something we have to remember. It is in the obscure heaviness within us that the "three distinct and complementary qualities" or *gunas*—the inert, dynamic, and subtle forces—give us a chance of a possible ascending movement because they are in constant interplay and motion. If it is easy to speak about a new state of consciousness, the only true work in depth is first to discover in oneself the existence of these "distinct and complementary qualities." They move constantly, always in the same order, just like the colors in the sky at dawn and at sunset, projecting us out of ourselves, in many different moods, in the midst of anger, jealousy, sadness, anguish, or exultation. The aim at any moment is to reach a luminous reality expressed by the unity of these qualities.

In the manifestation around us, it is very difficult to conceive that heavy and opaque matter, such as a clod of earth, can become as transparent as rock crystal. Similarly, if I feel myself a prisoner, it is due to the fact that I do not know what imprisons me. But the master is there to make it possible for the pupil to see, little by little, always by direct experience, how cosmic energy penetrates matter until it becomes itself inert, how this energy condenses, and how it ends by breaking all resistance and opens up a way for us toward light. Certainly our slavery exists. It is a fact because reality is composed not only of the three *gunas*—the inert, dynamic, and subtle forces within us—but also of the combination of impressions and movements (*samskaras*) coming from the outside that make up our life from the moment of our birth.

In this picture, the Spirit (*Purusha*), which is beyond time and our understanding, can do nothing for us. But the space between Spirit and Manifestation can take shape in time. Jacob's ladder is a beautiful illustration of that. In spiritual experience the movement up or down this ladder is always a shock. Every passage from one density of being to another density is a shock: from inertia to activity, from activity to subtlety; it always brings a moment of revolution and tumult. The characteristic of India to reject nothing, since all is reality, enters into play here. A holy man, just like any adventurer, will have to pass through the same stages of inner work and will have to live fully the transitions from one density to another, until the moment comes when there are no more differences between what is spirit and what is matter. The traditional image is that of a burning ember. Is it matter that burns or is it a cluster of flames symbolic of the spirit? This image portrays a phenomenon of visible transubstantiation at the heart of spiritual experience. Starting from this experience, the structure of Samkhya integrates itself into our daily life. If our lower nature remains a complex of the three known "qualities" always intermingled, the Samkhya admits the existence of a "quality of a different order," pure in itself, which one day will emerge at the summit of the being to give to it a taste of felicity.

For the students who lived at the hermitage, the daily life became very intense. The master watched us living and working, carried as we were by the waves of our own reactions and passions. Some of us were upset by what we discovered in ourselves. Then the master would say, "You have a fear of drowning. Why do you not swim in the direction of the temple of the heart? *There* is the seat of the immobile conscience."

But how can we reach it? The master would say, "Refuse to be the slave of your reactions. Have a deep desire to master them." At the same time, we would discover with his help that one cannot change the course of the manifestation, for every manifestation knows only its own law and does its own work without fail—it must run its course according to the needs of universal events. Immersed in it, governed by it, we cannot have full mastery of our own manifestation.

The conditions in which we lived were difficult. One could wish for nothing better than a hamlet in the Himalayas as a setting for the study of oneself. Apart from there being no easily available water or food supplies, there was no electricity, wood, telephone, medicine, or gasoline. The road, which was only a track, often disappeared in the rainy season. Every incident of life we experienced brought us to an observation of ourselves. What was it that was happening within each of us? The master said, "From the outside it is impossible to know if the driver of an ox cart has control or not. If he has, he stops the ox cart when he desires. It is due to him that the wheels turn. Similarly, he controls his personal manifestation, which plays a part in a manifestation much greater than his own; and there again, in their turn, the cosmic laws are playing their part in what is greater still. Perched on the shaft, the driver of the ox cart simultaneously sees the turning of two large wooden wheels; one is life, the other is death. The two wheels are equally necessary for the equilibrium of the cart."

In this concept of equilibrium there are two basic tendencies between the perfect law of manifestation, which is objective, and the manifestation of man trying step by step to become more conscious. One tendency leads him constantly to the level of the heavy manifestation, and the other leads him toward knowledge. We were asked to understand the complexity of being in order to learn how to be free of it. Our conversations with the master, in the evening, were entirely focused on the possibility of finding the necessary equilibrium to evaluate our discoveries. The "rebel" in each of us was unmasked in its self-expression. The master gave it a warm welcome, engaging us to recognize it in all its aspects.

We would often listen to the master speak of the concept of space-time, which, in the *spiritual existentialism* as we lived it around him, became the measure of existence in which everything was "astir without movement." He showed us how a seed suffices in itself, coiled on itself, containing the tree in its entirety: roots, trunk, branches, leaves, flowers, and fruits. Similarly, a grain of thought coiled around its energies can perceive the mystery of pure Existence (*sat*).[1] But for this work to be done, there is a need at first for a period of silence during which life is reduced to as little as possible, where, in spite of the impulse to go on, one is often slowed down by all that one carries with oneself, useless, heavy. Nevertheless, when one is consciously engaged on the way of search, one can no longer go backward. One text of the Bhagavata Purana tells the story of a crow who was flying with a piece of meat in its beak.

[1] *Sat-chit-ananda*, where *sat* stands for the Void.

Twenty crows were pursuing it trying to grab the meat. Flying high to escape them, it became tired. Suddenly, it dropped the meat, and the twenty crows flew down shrieking, fighting for it. Then the crow, flying high, thought, "How good it is to carry nothing—the whole sky belongs to me."

Up to the time when a certain equilibrium is reached, even in the midst of a desired discipline, it is normal that one has moments of attraction as well as moments of revolt. One of the most important attempts of Samkhya is to return voluntarily to the point where, for the first time, in the "quality of obscurity" of the ego, an act of conscious will has arisen, taking the form of a desire for knowledge. This permits the seeker to perceive that from that moment on, only the nourishment coming from the subtle part of the being has been of help. All that has come from the outside is erased.

But at the same time man keeps asking the same question: "Why? why?" He does this without realizing that he is putting himself in the role of an "accuser" of the manifestation of which he himself is only a part, a manifestation that includes his intelligence, spirit, and mind, and his own personal search. As long as he says "Why?" he cannot progress, because there is no logical answer to the primeval source of life. Only the question "How?" allows thoughts to become the seat of a passive experience with a very fine sensation of existence similar to the life that is hidden in a seed.

How much we needed the help of the master at this moment! We did not know how to live in the thought that would have enabled such an experience to sustain us. We continued to remain in the constant recurrences of the mechanical manifestation, lacking flexibility and lightness. The master continuously encouraged us by saying, "Lean only on yourself. Cultivate the direct experience you are living until it becomes a part of yourself. Do not disclose it to anyone before you can go to the very root of yourself."

When a pupil plunges into himself, he seems to lose his strength. But the master is there to protect him. Shri Anirvan sustained us by his presence hour by hour. We felt his presence in our midst, toiling with us in a surprising way. As a laborer, he worked eight hours each day to complete a task that he had set for himself. His task was to translate the Vedas into a language that could be understood by everyone. More than that, he carried the full burden of each of us. In accordance with the ancient tradition of masters in their schools of esoteric teaching, he accepted no money from his pupils. We were entirely dependent upon him during the period of our stay, which could last for a long time. Although there was no established rule, the pupil could send a gift after having left the master.

This experience of dependence—which was, for me, the most difficult to undergo—taught me with deep humility to abandon the "character" that I had imagined myself to be. Often, I awoke in the morning feeling that I had been watched while asleep. There were people from the hamlet or from the neighborhood who had entered my room and who had sat alongside the wall and watched me. Since they brought rice from their field, wheat, or some rupees to the master, and since I was living in the master's house, I belonged to them. They had rights on my thoughts and my attitude as well as rights to know what I was doing and where I was going. During all these years, my movements were watched. Everyone knew from where my letters came, to whom I was writing, and what I was eating. After having understood the deep reasons for this dependence and having accepted it—namely, to live before the eyes of each one—I felt supported by the sacrifice of these poor mountain people. Shri Anirvan himself, having given everything to me—his teaching, his strength, and his time—expected nothing from me in return. When I first arrived, he had said to me, "If in a glimpse, you once see what your real individuality is, why not try a discipline that leads toward the expansion of your inner being?" He gave me such a chance, an opportunity to seize all the circumstances of my life as the field of my personal research. After my departure, he followed from afar how my life was developing. Since then I have visited him several times. He continues to encourage me in the discipline I am following in Europe. Though he is now gravely ill, his mind is clear and alert. He sees what is beyond manifestation. He speaks of the connection which establishes itself in the Void—which is nothingness. "The Void," he says, "is that in which there are no more boundaries between what is in the conscious being and what is in the play of cosmic laws." At this point of understanding, Samkhya enables one "to follow the development of manifestation in which a rapid perception is sustained by a fine attention. At this point the ego vanishes."

The discipline of Samkhya accepts life just as it is, with all that it includes, as the point of departure. This life is precisely the arena where the play of cosmic laws takes place. In himself, man is a microcosm, an exact duplicate in miniature of the universal macrocosm that surrounds him. Man's opportunity is that, in the midst of Great Nature, of which he is a part, he can discover "what is free" within himself. But to reach this freedom there is a long road in the midst of all the contradictions hidden in his mind and heart.

In spite of the deep bond that has been established between the pupil and the master, a mute struggle is then inevitable between them. This is because the master can stimulate the pupil only by suggestion. To speak too soon would harm the pupil, as would giving too much manure to a young plant. On the other hand, the pupil is impatient with his own disorderly movements, passivity, and resentment. This struggle is part of the law of inner work; nothing can reduce it. It is simply the result of the moment when, in the midst of mechanical manifestation, "something which was inert becomes dynamic." The impersonal love of the master takes the form of patient waiting.

Samkhya speaks both of the state of sleep in which we live without being aware of it and of awakening. By ourselves we are unable to see the inner walls that imprison us, the heavy matter from which it is necessary to detach ourselves. When discovering the qualities and densities that characterize the depth of our being, we encounter, first, a deep sleep that is a form of stupor; second, a sleep filled with confusing elements; and, third, a sleep in which something has remained alert. Samkhya speaks, however, of a state of consciousness still more wide awake, a state in which everything parades before one's attention in such a way that a new discipline asserts itself, a voluntary effacement of oneself. This can be felt only in a deep "decontraction" with a very distinct feeling of self. This is a work to which the pupil is obliged to devote much attention. As the master says, "It is impossible to will to forget, but let a movement arise from the heart and mind to fill your whole being. At this moment, you are like a bell without a clapper filled by the vibration of a sound from nowhere."

Further, Samkhya attaches much importance to the work of interiorization; but, if it is to be of value, it must be guided with rigor. Shri Anirvan knew well our individual possibilities for following a plan of personal work on ourselves. Each one had accepted the idea of a personal discipline. This discipline started with a quieting of the body that was to help lead us from one level of being to another. We had to cross several empty spaces within us and each time a different chaotic movement was aroused. We came to discover our hidden fears and reactions, our recurring tendencies and habits, as well as our greediness, even when we thought these had all been conquered. As I found out later, this work, in all of its details, was leading us toward what in the Gurdjïeff teaching is called self-observation.

The first rule was to discover within ourselves what was dominant in terms of intellect, will, or feeling. To coordinate "what is within us" is a long and exacting work. Therefore, the master encouraged us not to hurry any of our actions, but to watch our thought rigorously before making any decisions. He said, "Be attentive to each thing that you do, since the smallest of them is the most important. This control will take its place, once and for all, as soon as you will be able to register the value of a fact in itself." In practical terms this meant to start from the "world such as it is," in order to reach the point of "what I know of myself in all its aspects." In this way I am brought back to "what is born in me and what is born with me," that is to say to the essence of my being. Here an instinctive honesty hinders deception; I know who I am. It was the entry into the discipline of real "self-remembering" that touched the source of our personal secret energy. When the master saw that we were ready to attempt such an effort, he added, "Stand on your own feet. Look at what you really are."

It is through this attitude of self-remembering that it is possible to become a responsible being, not by mutilating one's tendencies and thereby generating revenge in the future, but by making active what is now passive in us. Without fail the pupil who has undertaken such a discipline sees his own life and the life around him from a new angle. He sees in himself a multitude of "I's," each one with a different will. A rebellion would simply resemble the struggle of ants against an elephant. But seekers joined together can discover a new way of thinking from which it is possible to see the manifestation stirring both outside and within oneself, without being involved in it.

At the outset, theoretically at least, the permanent "I" within myself, which I think I know well and toward which all the "I's" of my personal tendencies converge, is the Void. The Void does exist. It can be understood and reached through the spiritual experience of the monistic Samkhya. The Void is within the ego, since the ego can vanish. It is the matrix of the universal energy from which all the laws of the cosmos that link us are born and to which they are brought back. It is also the luminous ether from which the sound originates, as well as the five elements that belong to creation in the descending law, and the five sensations that belong to man in the ascending law.

The master often said, "The best thing to do to become familiar with the idea of the Void is for a time not to act on one's own initiative but to observe what is happening. Let Great Nature unfold." The following paradox is revealing of the whole situation: If life is symbolized by a boat, it is necessary to hold fast to the rudder, to be one with it, to risk everything, without letting go. At the same time, it is necessary to know that everything is impermanent: the boat, the sea, and ourselves. At this moment, the movement of thought falls, there is only the "I" that perceives the Void and the sensation of the blood that beats in the veins. And that will be so until one day the "I" itself vanishes into the Void.

How did this crossing toward inner life work out in our little group? All discipline being accepted as a work of detail, each of us was deeply absorbed by his respective task. Shri Anirvan kept his "time for wandering" during the winter, going down to the plains from one city to another in northern India, where his pupils assembled around him for the period of his stay. For us, who remained at the hermitage, it was a time of seclusion without visitors, without noise from the outside. It was a time of reflection and for putting ourselves to a personal test. We waited for the letters from Shri Anirvan, who followed our inner work from afar. Sometimes his letters left a large backwash of reactions in their wake.

I have often been asked what place meditation had in our personal research. I should say that it was integrated in our life: it became a method of expansion and of penetration into all life which surrounded us, beings and things, with a precise sensation of passing from one element into another. We did not meditate as a group. Each of us received personal instructions. One day, perhaps after nine months at the hermitage, Shri Anirvan said to me, "I would like to accompany you until you realize a definite state of being. After that it will be necessary for you to leave." One evening, some four years later, I touched, alone, what he had described to me. My face was covered with tears. Rising to my feet, I thought, "I hope he will not guess it." But when we met, he saw immediately. Smiling with a great tenderness, he said, "Now it is necessary for you to return into the world, to accomplish your task. We all have a task. Activity is your yoga. A young tiger does not remain in the forest in

the shadow of a stronger one. He needs to have his own space. . . ."
I left the mountain some weeks later.

Meditation was a part of us. Each of us knew that meditation
could become the link between consciousness and the supreme reality
and could also transform the mental, vital, and even physical being.
At the same time the extreme relativity of consciousness and its lack
of continuity confused us. When the master was there, he sustained
our meditation because we did not know how to recognize in us the
active passivity that could bring us to a right inner movement.

At the beginning of meditation, all the thoughts were brought
back to our own body, to establish a contact with it, to feel its form
and weight, to establish a sensation of equilibrium until its stability
became a state in itself. Outwardly hard, the body becomes a pulsa-
tion of life, a flashing of light. The master said on occasion, "Meditation, to reach reality, is a personal laboratory work to help us escape
from the slavery of our manifestation. Be then attentive in recognizing your energies, learn to direct them, to make your decisions.
Nothing can be conceived in disorder, since the cosmic laws themselves exist only in a rigorously ordered scale of relativity."

Many people came to visit our small group of four to seven
people. Monks, refugees who had lost everything, even their own
identity, and frustrated politicians, including members of Parliament.
The chaos of the economic and political conditions of this period,
the problems of unemployment, overpopulation, hunger, and thirst,
provoked reactions of violence and noncollaboration. The greatest
ideas and the lowest instincts were all expressed. Our hermitage, on
the edge of the forest, was also the stage of another kind of war,
that of constant assaults of forces of Great Nature with a display
frightening to man. Winds from Tibet, storms, fires, earthquakes,
leopards, and panthers created around us a danger zone comparable
to the savage movements and upheavals in ourselves: "I want—I
don't want," "I like—I don't like," which tear the heart when they
occur.

The contrast with the living experience of the master made it
possible for us to see with our eyes, to hear with our ears, and to feel
to the very root of ourselves. It helped us to stand on the threshold
of the temple of the heart. This is where the mystic sees the Son of
Man who is the Son of God, and where the true seeker senses the
Void.

Such an attitude in life is a new birth. It implies a deep mastery of self, the taste of feeling responsible to oneself. It is an approach to the hidden mystery at the heart of all traditions.

QUESTIONS AND ANSWERS

Q: *Would you say something about the conditions of your life that brought you to the decision to go to India? Had you tried to find some answers to your questions in Europe and the West?*

REYMOND: Well, I must tell you that my initial aim was to translate Indian texts that were written in English but not known to the French public. After the war, however, when I saw how all things were mixed up here, I wanted to go to India, not exactly to search for a new religion, but to see how people, in the midst of their great difficulties, were living according to their scripture. And I was amazed to see the relationship there between the conditions of life and what was in their scriptures. And India became the place where I learned to be true to my own self and to my own demand. Coming back to the West, I understood the West much better because instead of going to India with what I had learned, which did not fit very often with the life around me, I was forced to place myself fully in the face of a feeling of what is truth. And there I recognized that Reality is everywhere the same.

Q: *I feel a need to trust something different in myself than I trust now. It's like a glimpse of another possibility. But how is it possible to approach that possibility?*

REYMOND: Of course, we need a trust within ourselves, to go to something truer. We have to see and recognize how everything is mixed up, how our feelings, thoughts, and desires do not follow any real aim. I cannot follow, I cannot be true to a mere part of myself.

There is a deep study to undertake. And that study will bring light and will clarify all that is possible within me and will help me to discover a higher purpose. If I have the feeling of going toward what I call evolution, I have to make the necessary steps to clarify what is dark and obscure within me, and to make what is now passive become active and of full strength. It's a long study, but it brings us to really feel our place in that larger macrocosm of which we are a part.

Q: You spoke of the fact that the true seeker who says "yes" is a born poet and that poetry plays the role of the science of transmutation. In light of that, could you say something about the psychological functions of expression and discretion, and the poise between the two of them.

REYMOND: It's quite a question you are asking. If I could give you an answer in a few sentences it would be absolutely marvelous, because within ourselves even the movement of a thought going from mind to heart would be a real transmutation. It would be going from a thought to a feeling and from a feeling to a sensation, feeling myself. Then I would understand the whole world. I would understand the meaning of a relationship between myself and others, a relationship without failure. That's what we're really aiming at—what we can aim at.

Sufism and the Spiritual Needs of Contemporary Man

Seyyed Hossein Nasr

. . .

.

IN ORDER TO understand sacred tradition and to discuss the truth in its metaphysical sense, there must be not only interest and need but the aid of Heaven and the presence of a discerning intelligence. It is, therefore, necessary at the outset to turn an eye to the meaning of the theme of this book—namely, "sacred tradition and present need" and to discuss with discernment what "tradition" and "present need" signify.

By tradition we do not mean habit or custom or the automatic transmission of ideas and motifs from one generation to another. But, following the lead of such authors as F. Schuon, R. Guénon, and A. K. Coomaraswamy, we understand by tradition a set of principles rooted in Heaven and identified at their origin with a particular manifestation of the Divine—together with the application and deployment of these principles at different moments of time and in different sets of conditions for a particular segment of humanity. Tradition is therefore already sacred and the term "sacred tradition" is in a sense a pleonasm. Moreover, tradition is both immutable and a living continuity, containing within itself the science of Ultimate Reality and the means for the actualization and realization of this knowledge at different moments of time and space. To quote Schuon, "Tradition is not a childish and outmoded mythology but a science that is terribly real."[1] Tradition is ultimately a sacred science, a *scientia sacra*, rooted in the nature of Reality, and is the only integral means of access to this Reality, which at once surrounds man and shines at the innermost center of his being.

As far as Sufism itself is concerned, it should not, strictly speaking, be classified along with other integral traditions such as Hinduism and Buddhism, because Sufism is itself a part of the Islamic tradi-

---

[1] F. Schuon, *Understanding Islam*, trans. by D. M. Matheson (London, 1963); also in the Penguin Metaphysical Library, ed. by J. Needleman (Baltimore, 1972), p. ii.

tion. Islam can be spoken of as a tradition in the same way as one speaks of Christianity or Buddhism, whereas Sufism must be understood as a dimension of the Islamic tradition. This rather obvious point needs to be emphasized because today Sufism is often taken out of its Islamic context and then discussed along with other Oriental or Occidental traditions.

Sufism is actually like the flower of the tree of Islam, and in another sense the sap of that tree. Or it can be called the jewel in the crown of the Islamic tradition. But whatever image is used, it is undeniable that Sufism, taken out of the context of Islam, could not be fully understood and its methods could never be practiced efficaciously, to say the least. Nor, on the other hand, could one do justice to the wholeness of the Islamic tradition and its immensely rich spiritual possibilities by putting aside its inner dimension, which is Sufism.[2] In speaking about Sufism, therefore, we shall in reality be speaking about the Islamic tradition itself in its most inward and universal aspect.

As for the question of present need, which forms the second part of the title of this book, it is essential to analyze fully the content and meaning of this expression with respect to the cloud of illusion that surrounds modern man and makes the clear discernment of his environment and "living space," both external and internal, well-nigh impossible. There has been so much talk during the past century about change, becoming, and evolution that the permanent and abiding inner nature of man has been nearly forgotten, along with the most profound needs of this inner man. In fact the pseudo-dogma of evolution, as generally understood, which continues to dominate the horizon of much of modern anthropology and philosophy in the teeth of rapidly accumulating evidence concerning the essentially unchanged nature of man during the many millennia that have passed since his entering upon the stage of terrestrial history, has made it impossible for those who adhere to it to understand who man is.[3] Moreover, the permanent nature of man having

[2] For the relationship between Sufism and the rest of the Islamic tradition see F. Schuon, op. cit., chapter 4; F. Schuon, The Transcendent Unity of Religions, trans. by P. Townsend (London, 1953, and New York, 1975); S. H. Nasr, Ideals and Realities of Islam (London, 1966, and Boston, 1972), chapter 1.

[3] See S. H. Nasr, The Encounter of Man and Nature, the Spiritual Crisis of Modern Man (London, 1968), pp. 124–29; also S. H. Nasr, "Man in the Universe," in I Valori Permanenti nel Divenire Storico (Rome, 1969), pp. 287–98; also in S. H. Nasr, Sufi Essays (London, 1972), chapter 6.

been forgotten, the needs of man are reduced to the sphere of accidental changes that affect only the outer crust of man's being.

In reality, the needs of man, as far as the total nature of man is concerned, remain forever the same, precisely because of man's unchanging nature. "Man is what he is, or he is nothing."[4] The situation of man in the universal hierarchy of being, his standing between the two unknowns that comprise his state before terrestrial life and his state after death, his need for a "shelter" in the vast stretches of cosmic existence, and his deep need for certainty (*yaqīn* in the parlance of Sufism) remain unchanged. This last element—the need to gain certainty—is in fact so fundamental that the Sufis have described the stages of gaining spiritual perfection as so many steps in the attainment of certainty.[5]

The very fact that there is so much interest today in Oriental metaphysics and spirituality in the West is indirectly proof of the fact that there is a profounder nature in man that does not "evolve," a nature whose needs remain unchanged. This more permanent nature may be temporarily eclipsed, but it cannot be permanently obliterated. The rationalistic philosophers of the eighteenth and nineteenth centuries never dreamed that a century or two later so many people in the Western world would again become interested in religion and even in the occult sciences, which in their unadulterated form are applications of the traditional cosmological sciences. These men would be surprised to discover that the works of Taoist sages or the rishis of India or Sufi masters would soon be read more avidly than their own writings. They regarded only the outer crust of man's being, and they saw in its condensation and consolidation, its gradual separation from the world of the Spirit, a progress and evolution that they thought to be a continual process. They did not see that the crust would break of its own accord as a result of the advancement of the very process of its solidification and that the needs of the inner man would manifest themselves once again on the scale we see before us today.

---

[4] F. Schuon, "The Contradiction of Relativism," *Studies in Comparative Religion*, Spring, 1973, p. 70.

[5] Usually three stages of certainty are distinguished, based upon the language of the Qur'ān: "the knowledge of certainty" (*'ilm al-yaqīn*), "the eye of certainty" (*'ayn al-yaqīn*), and the "truth of certainty" (*ḥaqq al-yaqīn*). These three stages have been compared to hearing a description of fire, seeing fire, and being burned in fire. See Abū Bakr Sirāj ed-Dīn, *The Book of Certainty* (London, 1952).

It was once asked of the Prophet of Islam what existed before Adam. He answered, "Adam." The question was repeated. He again answered "Adam" and added that if he were to answer this question to the end of time he would repeat, "Adam." The profound meaning of this *hadīth* (saying of the Prophet of Islam) is that man in his essential reality has not undergone evolution and that there is no "before man" in the sense of a temporal predecessor and a state from which man developed "in time." Already a million years ago men buried their dead and believed in the Invisible World.[6] Over ten thousand years ago man not only produced masterpieces of art but even described the motion of the heavens in a most remarkable manner in myths and stories that reveal a "power of abstraction" that could match any of the feats of men of later periods of history.[7]

It is this man, obliterated temporarily by the progressive and evolutionary theories of the past few centuries in the West, to whom tradition addresses itself, and it is this inner man that tradition seeks to liberate from the imprisonment of the ego and the suffocating influence of the purely externalized and forgetful aspect of man. Moreover, it is tradition alone that possesses the means for his liberation, and not the pseudo-religions so prevalent today that, seeing the resurgence of the needs of the inner man, try to entice those with a less discerning eye by means of parodies of the teachings of the sacred traditions, to which they almost invariably add something of the evolutionary pseudo-philosophy to make sure men do not discover who they really are. But that inner man continues to reside within men's being no matter how far they seek to escape from their own center and no matter what means they use to obliterate the traces of the inner man upon what they call "themselves."

Of course when all is said concerning the permanent needs of man—needs which in fact must be emphasized in the strongest terms possible because they have been so forgotten in the modern world—it must be remembered that these needs concern only one pole of man's being, although the essential pole. But as far as the other pole is concerned—the pole that involves man's temporality and the historico-cultural conditions that color the outer crust of his being—it can be said that man's needs *have* changed. They have changed not in their essence but in their mode and external form.

[6] See J. Servier, *L'homme et l'invisible* (Paris, 1964).
[7] See G. Di Santillana and E. von Dechend, *Hamlet's Mill* (New York, 1967).

Even in traditional societies, which are based on immutable transcendent principles, the form in which the spiritual needs have been fulfilled has varied from culture to culture. So much more is this true in the modern world, where men live in a desacralized milieu divorced from principles, where the psyche is separated from the Spirit which is its source of life, where the experience of time and space, not to speak of all kinds of human relations, have been completely altered, and where the sense of authority has gradually disappeared. In such conditions there appear new modes through which even the deepest human needs must be fulfilled.

The very process of the consolidation of the world has introduced cracks in the closed system of materialism that permit not only the dark forces from below to enter into the world but also light from above. This process implies at the same time a reawakening of man to his real needs, which leads naturally to a desperate attempt to find means of fulfilling these needs. But precisely because of the changed external conditions, many modern men do not understand or are not willing to undergo the sacrifices necessary to become worthy of receiving the message of Heaven, which in its unadulterated form is contained only within the living orthodox and sacred traditions of the world. Also, many authorities from these traditions—not to speak of the pretenders who have recently flooded the scene—habituated to the traditional world from which they have issued, are not aware of the differences existing within the psyche of Western man and do not see the different forms that his spiritual needs take because of the particular type of world that has nurtured him.

In speaking of present needs, it is essential to keep in mind both these poles—namely, the permanent nature of man's needs, which makes all the traditional teachings about man and his final end pertinent and vital, and the changed form of man's needs owing to the particular experiences of modern man. It must be remembered that traditional authority and authenticity must be preserved, that truth cannot evolve, that it is man who must make himself worthy of becoming the recipient of the message of Heaven, not *vice versa*, that truth cannot be distorted to suit the passing whims and fashions of a particular period,[8] and that there is an objective reality that determines the value of a man's thoughts and actions,

[8] See R. Guénon, *The Reign of Quantity and the Signs of the Times*, trans. by Lord Northbourne (Baltimore, 1972).

and finally judges them and determines his mode of existence in the world to come. At the same time it must be recalled that this sacred tradition must be applied to the particular problems and conditions of modern man without destroying its authenticity and without turning application into distortion. The modern world is witness to an array of men and organizations that attempt to cater to the spiritual needs of modern man, from authentic masters and organizations from the East that are not aware of the particular nature of the audience they are addressing[9] to the rare few who have succeeded in applying traditional teachings to the particular conditions of modern man[10] to the vast number of pseudo-masters and dubious organizations, ranging from the innocuous to the veritably satanical, which remind one of the saying of Christ about the false prophets arising at the end of time. To draw from the resources of sacred tradition to fulfill present needs is to remain totally within the matrix of sacred tradition and at the same time to apply its methods and teachings to a world in which people's needs are at once perennial and conditioned by the particular experiences of modern man.

An important condition that has deeply colored the mental processes of modern man, and today lies at the heart of the new religious movement in the West, is Cartesian dualism and the reaction that has set in against materialism within the context of this dualism. Cartesian dualism divided reality into the material and the mental, positing a nonmaterial substance that somehow engulfed all the

[9] We have in mind many spiritual masters and their spiritual organizations that have come to the West in the past few decades and sought to increase their following by disseminating exactly the same techniques and methods to Westerners that they were applying back in the East, with the result that many people unqualified for initiation have been allowed to practice methods that have been either fruitless or harmful to them and in certain cases have led to insanity. Many authentic *bhakti* masters from India have spread their message to Western disciples as if they were addressing a traditional Hindu audience. The results of such efforts are clear for all to see. In any case the tree is judged by the fruit it bears. Such cases must, however, be clearly distinguished from the self-proclaimed masters who do not issue from any orthodox traditional background but have the audacity to place themselves "above" traditional teachings and the perennial truths expounded by saints and sages throughout the centuries.

[10] The whole group of traditional writers in the Western world, consisting of such men as F. Schuon, R. Guénon, A. K. Coomaraswamy, M. Pallis, and T. Burckhardt, belongs to this category and for this reason plays a role of outstanding importance in the spiritual and religious life of the modern world even if their works have been neglected in many circles until recently.

levels of nonmaterial existence and reduced them to a single reality. The excessive materialism of the past centuries has now led many people to a rejection of materialism. But just as in physics a reaction is opposed to an existing action, so this philosophical and religious reaction has also set in within the already existing framework of the classical Cartesian dualism. For a large number of people the reaction against materialism means almost unconsciously an attraction toward the other substance of Cartesian dualism—namely, the nonmaterial. But this occurs without there being any discrimination between the spirit and the psyche, the *rūḥ* and the *nafs* of Sufism. Hence for many people psychic phenomena have come to replace the spiritual and the religious.

Islam teaches that the rebellion against God takes place on the level of the psyche, not of the body. The flesh is only an instrument for the tendencies originating within the psyche. It is the psyche that must be trained and disciplined so as to become prepared for its wedding with the Spirit. Both the angelic and the demonic forces manifest themselves in this intermediate plane of the psyche, which is neither purely material nor purely spiritual. The paradisiacal and infernal states refer to the macrocosmic counterparts of the various levels of this intermediate substance, which in the microcosm or man stretches from the corporeal to the divine center within the heart of man. Therefore, to identify all that is nonmaterial with the religious or spiritual is sheer folly and is a result of the optical illusion lingering from the delimitation of reality into two domains by Cartesian dualism. But it is an error that is very prevalent in the new religious movements of today, an error that in certain cases can open the soul of man to the most infernal influences. Simply to identify the nonmaterial with the spiritual is to misunderstand the nature of reality, the complexity of the human soul, the source and reality of evil, and the spiritual work necessary to reach the fountain of life which alone can satisfy the spiritual needs of man in a permanent and not illusory and transient manner.

This mistaking the psychic for the spiritual, so characteristic of our times, is reinforced by another powerful tendency issuing from man's need to break the boundaries of his limited world of experience. The Sufis have always taught that man is in quest of the Infinite and that even his endless effort toward the gaining of material possessions and his lack of satisfaction with what he has is an echo of this thirst, which cannot be quenched by that which is finite. That is why the Sufis consider the station of satisfaction (*riḍā'*)[11] as an exalted spiritual condition attainable only by those who have reached the "proximity" of the Infinite and have shed the bonds of finite existence. This need to seek the Infinite and overcome the limits of whatever is finite is clearly discernible in the new religious ferment today. Many modern men are tired of the finite psychic experiences of everyday life no matter how materially comfortable that life might be. Having no access to the authentic spiritual experience that in traditional societies provides the natural means of breaking the limits of finite existence, they turn to psychic experiences of all kinds, which open for them new worlds and horizons, even if they be infernal. The great concern with psychic phenomena, "trips," extraordinary "experiences," and the like is deeply related to this inner urge to break the suffocating and limited world of everyday life in a civilization that has no purpose beyond moving with accelerated speed toward an illusory ideal state of material well-being that is always just around the corner.

This tendency, added to the one that unconsciously identifies the noncorporeal with the spiritual, has succeeded in bringing about a most dangerous confusion in the religious life of modern man in the West and particularly in America, where the need for a rediscovery of the world of the spirit is most keenly felt. From the Sufi point of view, which has always distinguished clearly between the psychic and the spiritual, so many of those who claim to speak in the name of the Spirit today are really speaking in the name of the psyche and are taking advantage of the thirst of modern man for something beyond the range of experiences that modern, industrial civilization has made possible for him. It is precisely this confusion that lies at the heart of the profound spiritual disorder one observes in the West today, and that enables elements that are as far as possible removed from the sacred to absorb the energies even of men with good intentions, and to dissipate rather than integrate their psychic forces.

The sacred, as already stated, is related to the world of the Spirit and not the psyche. It is whole and holy; it illuminates and integrates rather than causing men to wander aimlessly through the labyrinth that characterizes the psychic and mental worlds whenever these worlds are deprived of the light of the Spirit. The sacred, precisely because it comes from God, asks of us all that we are. To

[11] Concerning this spiritual station, see S. H. Nasr, *Sufi Essays*, chapter 5.

sacralize life and to reach the sacred we must become ourselves sacred, like a sacred work of art. We must chisel out of the substance of our soul an icon that will reveal us as we really *are* in the Divine Presence, as we were when we were created, the *imago dei*; for as the Prophet of Islam has said, "God created man upon His own image." In order for man to become this work of art, to become him*self* again, he must surrender and dedicate himself fully to the commands of the Spirit, to the sacred. It is only the sacred that *can* enable man to remove the veil that hides his true being from himself and makes him forget his own theomorphic nature. And it is only the sacred, which comes from the Spirit and not the psyche, that can be the source of ethics, of aesthetics in its traditional sense, of metaphysical doctrine, and of methods of realization. The psyche may be fascinating or absorbing. But in itself it is always no more than amorphous, with impressions that are transitory and partial. It is only the spiritual or the sacred that is permanent and total and that, precisely because of its totality, embraces the psyche and even the corporeal aspects of man and transforms and illuminates them.

The application of sacred tradition—whether it be Sufism or something else—to the actual needs of man cannot begin at a more critical point than at this present junction of human history. Here it can provide the means of discerning between the spiritual and the psychic and by extension between those whose teachings are of a truly spiritual nature and those whose message is rooted only in the psychic and supported solely by psychic phenomena, related to experiences which without the protective matrix of sacred tradition can lead to the most infernal depths of cosmic existence and to states that are much more dangerous to the soul of man than various forms of crass materialism.

With regard to the Sufi tradition itself, it must be said that its understanding, like that of many other traditions, is made difficult in the modern West and especially in America because of the presence of another optical illusion that mistakes the mental understanding of metaphysics for the full realization of its truths. This illusion, which is the result of the separation between the mental activity of certain types of men and the rest of their being and which is directly related to a lack of spiritual virtues, is a major hindrance in the application of the sacred teachings of various traditions to the present needs of man. There are those who possess intellectual intuition, itself a gift of Heaven, and who can understand the doctrines of Sufism or other forms of Oriental metaphysics, but who are not willing to live their lives in accordance with the teachings of the sacred tradition whose flower they are able to scent from far away.[12] Such people confuse the vision of the mountain peak, *theoria* in its original sense, with actually being at the summit of the mountain. They therefore tend to belittle all the practical, moral, and operative teachings of tradition as being below their level of concern. Most of all, they mistake the emphasis upon the attainment of spiritual virtues (*faḍāʾil* in Sufism) for sentimentality, and faith (*īmān*) for "common religion" belonging only to the exoteric level,[13] forgetting that the greatest saints and sages have spoken most of all of spiritual virtues and that one of the most widely used names for Sufism is Muhammadan poverty (*al-faqr al-muḥammadī*).[14]

This prevalent error, noticeable also in the present day "religious landscape," is related to the anomalous situation of our times in which the purest metaphysical teachings of various traditions are easily available in translation for just a few dollars at every book store—works ranging from the Song of Solomon to the *Tao Te-Ching*. Obviously, such has never been the case in a normal situation. In a traditional society most of those drawn to the meta-

---

[12] "Metaphysical knowledge is one thing; its actualization in the mind quite another. All the knowledge which the brain can hold, even if it is immeasurably rich from a human point of view, is as nothing in the sight of Truth. As for metaphysical knowledge, it is like a divine seed in the heart; thoughts are only very faint glimmers from it." F. Schuon, *Spiritual Perspectives and Human Facts*, trans. by D. M. Matheson (London, 1952), p. 9.

[13] For the role of "faith" in the realization of the highest metaphysical truths, see F. Schuon, "The Nature and Arguments of Faith," in *Stations of Wisdom*, trans. by G. E. H. Palmer (London, 1961), p. 52 ff.

[14] The great Algerian saint of this century, Shaykh Aḥmad al-ʿAlawī, often repeated the Sufi saying, "He whose soul melteth not away like snow in the hand of religion, in his hand religion like snow away doth melt" (trans. by M. Lings in his *A Sufi Saint of the Twentieth Century* [London, 1971]). This dictum is a direct allusion to the need for man's separative existence to melt away in the Truth through the attainment of the virtues, which are the only way in which the truth can become actualized in the being of man. Despite the emphasis upon this basic feature of all authentic spirituality by masters of old, as well as by the leading present-day exponents of traditional doctrines such as F. Schuon and T. Burckhardt, there has now formed a whole group of "traditionalists" in the West who accept the teachings of tradition mentally but who do not find it necessary to practice the disciplines of an authentic way and to discipline their souls in order to become themselves embodiments of the Truth. It is in their case that the second part of the saying of Shaykh al-ʿAlawī applies, for religion or truth simply melts away in their hands instead of becoming actualized in their being.

physical and gnostic aspects of their tradition are attracted through gradual instruction, which prepares them for the reception of gnostic doctrines only after long training. Moreover, their knowledge of tradition is through personal contact. They live the exoteric form of the tradition, which is absolutely necessary and indispensable, in their everyday lives and they contact esotericism most often by encountering a master or his disciples, or by visiting the tomb of a saint, or by having a dream that incites them to seek a particular master or go to a particular place. Even when their contact with esotericism is through reading, it is most often through literature and parables that gradually arouse their interest in the Way. For a thousand people in the Islamic world who read the poetry of Ḥāfiẓ or Rūmī only one or two read the purely doctrinal treatises of Sufism.

Today in the West there is a truly anomalous situation in which the contact of most men with tradition must of necessity begin from the top and through the channel of the written word or books, which play a special role in an age when the usual channels of oral transmission have become blocked in so many parts of the world. As a matter of fact, the very availability of the highest metaphysical teachings of not one but most of the sacred traditions today—not to speak of the remarkable expositions of the authentic traditional writers in the West—is a result of the divine mercy, which has made possible this compensation during an age of spiritual eclipse, inasmuch as one irregularity deserves another. But the danger in this situation consists precisely in mistaking the mental understanding of a sacred text, which one might chance upon, for the living of a tradition, which involves not only the mind but the whole of man's being.

With this reservation, it must be added that even on the plane of the mind the presence of expositions of traditional doctrines, whether they be of a metaphysical or cosmological order, can fulfill one of the deepest needs of modern man, who can be characterized as a being who thinks too much and often wrongly. Even a mental understanding of traditional doctrines can, therefore, be like a blanket of snow that brings with it peace and calm and quiets the agitation of the skeptical and questioning mind. It can bestow "the science of certainty" (*'ilm al-yaqīn*) upon man and therefore make him aware of the fact that the ultimate aim of knowledge is not to collect an ever-increasing number of facts and to charter areas *beyond* the present "frontiers" of knowledge but to reach the center and to gain a vision of or even become the knowledge that has always been and will always be. This calming of the agitated mind by providing answers to questions posed by reason, answers that are the fruits of revelation, illumination, or intellection, then provides the necessary background for the actual illumination of the mind of the being of him whose reason has been nourished by traditional knowledge rather than being left to its own machinations.[15]

With respect to the importance of doctrinal works in this process of calming the mind and preparing the person of a contemplative bent for true intellection, it is unfortunate that as far as Islamic metaphysics is concerned few of its riches in this domain have been translated into English, in comparison with what one finds from Hindu, Buddhist, and Taoist sources. A few of the greatest masterpieces of Islamic metaphysics, such as the *Fuṣūṣ al-ḥikam* of Ibn ʿArabī and *al-Insān al-kāmil* of al-Jīlī, are now known and partially translated,[16] but a vast treasury of works by both Sufis and Islamic theosophers such as Suhrawardī, Ibn Turkah al-Iṣfahānī, Mīr Dāmād, and Mullā Ṣadrā, who have composed major doctrinal and metaphysical treatises, remains almost completely inaccessible to a Westerner not possessing a reading knowledge of Arabic or Persian.[17]

[15] "In knowledge, reasoning can play no part other than that of being the occasional cause of intellection: intellection will come into play suddenly—not continuously or progressively—as soon as the mental operation, which was in its turn conditioned by an intellectual intuition, has the quality which makes of it a pure symbol." F. Schuon, *Spiritual Perspectives and Human Facts*, p. 13.

[16] Thanks to the efforts of T. Burckhardt, there are excellent summaries with precious notes of both of these works in French—*La sagesse des prophètes* (Paris, 1955), and *De l'homme universel* (Lyon, 1953). Burckhardt has also summarized the doctrinal teachings of the school of Ibn ʿArabī in his *Introduction to Sufi Doctrine*, trans. by D. M. Matheson (London, 1959). In English there are also several partial translations of Sufi doctrinal works, including *Studies in Islamic Mysticism* by R. A. Nicholson (Cambridge, 1919), which contains a translation of parts of al-Jīlī's al-Insān al-kāmil, and several translations by A. J. Arberry of al-Kalābādhī, Ibn al-Fāriḍ, and others. What is needed, however, is complete translations into English of these and the many other works of those Sufi masters who have given an open exposition of Sufi doctrine.

[17] As far as this school of theosophy (*al-ḥikmat al-ilāhiyyah*) and its importance for an understanding of Islamic metaphysics are concerned, see S. H. Nasr, *Three Muslim Sages* (Cambridge, Mass., 1964), chapter 2; Nasr, "The School of Isfahan" and "Ṣadr al-Dīn Shīrāzi," in M. M. Sharif (ed.), *A History of Muslim Philosophy*, vol. 2 (Wesbaden, 1966), and the many works of H. Corbin, who has devoted a lifetime to making this as-yet little-known aspect of Islamic intellectual and spiritual life better known in the West. See especially his *En Islam Iranian*, 4 vols. (Paris, 1971–72). He has also translated one of the major treatises of Mullā Ṣadrā into French as *Le livre des pénétrations métaphysiques* (Tehran-Paris, 1964).

In this way the application of the teachings of Islam in its esoteric and metaphysical aspects to present-day needs is handicapped by a lack of well-translated material that would make the vast treasures of this tradition accessible to those capable of reaping their fruit. And also the true appreciation of all that the Islamic tradition can offer to contemporary man has become difficult, for, whereas in the case of other traditions their most universal teachings are relatively well known, in the case of Islam most studies available in Western languages have been devoted to its legalistic and formal aspects, while its universal aspect has not received the necessary attention.

Some who seek to follow a tradition today are in fact fooled by this situation into thinking that Islam is concerned only with law, divine justice and punishment, rigor, and so on, while it is possible to follow other traditions by simply reading their gnostic treatises, or even by pulling some particular initiatory practice out of context and practicing it, without having to be burdened with moral considerations or questions of divine justice and punishment. Actually, this is a most unfortunate modern delusion, due to the fact that, as a result of a reaction against an unintelligible moralism within certain forms of modern Christianity, many people today belittle the importance of morality, and as a result of the rebellion of modern man against Heaven and the loss of the meaning of authority, the importance of the fear of God in religious life has been well-nigh forgotten. The prophetic utterance, "Fear of God is the beginning of wisdom" (*ra's al-ḥikmah makhāfat Allāh*), which echoes the well-known Pauline dictum, holds true not only for Islam and Christianity but for all traditions. In Islam there is a Divine Law (*Sharī'ah*) that concerns man's actions and that all Muslims— Sufis or non-Sufis—must follow.[18] There is also emphasis upon the fear of God and an eschatology related to God's judgment of human action on earth. But then these elements are also present in other forms in Hinduism and other Oriental traditions. Hinduism has not only produced the *Gita* and the *Vedanta* but also elaborate treatises on *pralaya*, the last judgment, and on *karma* and the serious consequences of human action on earth for man's posthumous states. It would be the worst illusion to imagine that one can practice, let us say, Yoga and forget all about morality or the consequences of human acts in the eyes of God simply because one has moved from one

---

[18] See S. H. Nasr, *Ideals and Realities of Islam*, chapter 4.

tradition to another. Actually, in every tradition one can find the fear, the love, and the knowledge of God. As al-Ghazzālī has said, he who fears the Creator runs toward Him and loves Him, and he who loves Him knows Him.

The historic manifestations of Sufism reveal the phases of fear (makhāfah), love (maḥabbah), and knowledge (maʿrifah), and the cycle repeats itself within the soul of every man who gains spiritual realization. If one can complain from one point of view that the gnostic and metaphysical works of Islam have not been translated widely enough, one can be thankful from another point of view that the integral teachings of Islam, including the Sharīʿah, are there to test the seriousness of those who would aspire to reach its inner chamber, by requiring them to become aware of the Divine Majesty that creates in man an awe and fear that is absolutely positive and that melts away from the substance of the soul that which is alien to its primordial nature.

In fact, it is in order to evade this test and this protecting criterion that recently pretenders have appeared in the West who wish to divorce Sufism from Islam and present it as if it had nothing to do with the teachings of Islam and its Sharīʿah, which provides the divine matrix for human action and protects the person who follows it from the wrath of God. This effort is no more than sheer delusion. In all authentic manifestations of Sufism the fear of God, as described so majestically in the Qurʾān and incorporated in the attitudes promulgated by the Sharīʿah, prepares the ground for the love of God, and the love of God in turn leads to gnosis or the knowledge of God, which cannot sink its roots into the being of man unless the soil of his being has been prepared for such a divine plant by the fear of God and His love, a love that in Islamic spirituality always accompanies knowledge.

So far most of what has been said concerns all traditions. But what is unique about Sufism itself as it concerns the present needs of man? There is an Arabic saying that states, "The doctrine of unity is unique" (al-tawḥīd wāḥid). This means that at the highest level there is only one truth, in which all traditions are unified. But as the divine Truth descends from the one peak downward toward men it takes on the characteristics that distinguish one tradition from another.

Being the inner dimension of Islam, Sufism shares in its formal aspect in the particular features of this tradition. Since Islam is based on unity (*al-tawḥīd*), all its manifestations reflect unity in one way or another—most of all Sufism, in which the principles of the revelation are most directly reflected. The presence of the principle of Unity in Sufism means, among other things, that its methods and practices unify what in other traditions is usually separate and distinct. To use the terminology of Hinduism—which is a miracle on the religious plane because of the different spiritual forms that have existed within it—the way of *karma* (action) Yoga, *bhakti* (love) Yoga, and *jñani* (knowledge) Yoga are combined in Sufism into a single way, one might say into an "integral Yoga." It is especially important to note that whereas in Hinduism the *jñani* and *bhakti* types are quite distinct, Sufi spirituality is essentially a *jñani* one which, however, is never divorced from the element of *bhakti*. Some Sufis might emphasize one aspect more than another. Some, such as Ibn 'Arabī and Shabistarī, might speak more of gnosis (*ma'rifah*) and some, such as Aṭṭār and Ḥāfiẓ, of love. But in no instance does one find in Sufism a path of knowledge completely separated from love or a path of love without the element of gnosis, such as the type of love mysticism found in Christianity and also in medieval Hinduism. Moreover, this combination of knowledge and love in Sufism is always based on the support of the *Sharī'ah*, or in a sense, on a way of work or action.

Because of the unitive nature of the Islamic revelation, the contemplative and active ways have never been totally separated either outwardly or inwardly in Sufism. There is no outward monasticism in Islam, and the most intense contemplative life in Islam is carried out within the matrix of life within society. The Sufi has died to the world inwardly while outwardly he still participates in the life of society and bears the responsibilities of the station of life in which destiny has placed him.

In fact, he performs the most perfect action because his acts emanate from an integrated will and an illuminated intelligence. Rather than being in any way contradictory, the contemplative and active lives complement each other in all Islamic spirituality,[19] and the methods and techniques of the contemplative life are such that they can be performed in whatever outward circumstances a person may find himself and in whichever form of active life he might have to participate.

[19] See S. H. Nasr, "The Complementarity of Contemplation and Action in Islam," *Main Currents of Modern Thought*, December, 1973.

This unitive character of Sufism, both in its own methods and its relation to man's outward life in society, offers obvious advantages for men living in the modern world, where inner withdrawal is usually more of a possibility than outward separation from the world. Also, the unitive nature of Sufism is a powerful remedy for the disintegrated life from which so many people in the modern world suffer. The total integration of the personality achieved in Sufi training is the goal sought by much of psychotherapy and psychoanalysis, which, however, can never achieve this goal because these methods are cut off from the grace of the Spirit, which alone can integrate the psyche.

The pertinent question that will undoubtedly be asked is, granted that Sufism does contain these characteristics, what are the possibilities of practicing it? Of course one cannot gauge the mercy of Heaven, for the "spirit bloweth where it listeth," but as far as the traditional teachings of Sufism are concerned, it is always emphasized that there is no practice of Sufism possible except through a master, who is referred to traditionally as *shaykh*, *murshid*, or *pīr*. The only exception is that of special individuals (*afrād*) who are disciples of the ever-living but hidden prophet *Khaḍir*[20] and who are chosen for the way by Heaven. But this possibility is not an option for man to choose. As far as the aspirant is concerned the only way open to him is to find an authentic master. The question of the practical possibility of living according to the disciplines of Sufism, therefore, comes down essentially to the possibility of finding an authentic master.

Here it is necessary to mention the danger of false masters, of those who pretend to be guides without possessing the necessary qualifications, which are given by God alone. Even in classical times, when the danger of "false prophets" mentioned by Christ was much less than in these late hours of human history, authentic masters took care to warn against the dangers of submitting oneself to an un-

[20] Khaḍir, who corresponds to Elias, symbolizes the esoteric function in the story of Khaḍir and Moses in the Qur'an and is usually represented as the "green prophet." See A. K. Coomaraswamy, "Khwaja Khadir and the Fountain of Life, in the Tradition of Persian and Mughal Art," *Studies in Comparative Religion*, Vol. 4, Autumn 1970, pp. 221–30. In Shi'ite Islam the Twelfth Iman fulfills a similar function and in Sufism in general the Uwaysīs are a particular order who are said to receive initiation from the "invisible master." See also the numerous studies of L. Massignon on the spiritual significance of Khaḍir, for example, "Elie et son rôle transhistorique, Khadirīya, en Islam," *Etudes carmélitaines: Elie la prophète* (Paris, 1956), Vol. 2, pp. 269–90.

qualified "master." In his incomparable *Mathnawī*, Jalāl al-Dīn Rūmī says:

پس بهرد ستی نشاید داد دست   چون بسی ابلیس آدم روی هست

تا بخواند برسلیمی زان فســـون   حرف درویشان بد زد د مرد د ون

کارد ونان حیله وبی شرمی است   کارمردان روشنی وگرمی اســـت

بومسیلم را لقب احمد کننـــد   جامه پشمین ازبرای که کننـــد

باد ه را ختمش بود گند وعـــذاب   آن شراب حق ختامش مشك ناب

Since there is many a devil who hath the face of Adam, it is not well to give your hand to every hand. . . .[21]

The vile man will steal the language of dervishes, that he may thereby chant a spell over [fascinate and deceive] one who is simple.

The work of [holy] men is [as] light and heat, the work of vile men is trickery and shamelessness.

They make a woolen garb for the purpose of begging. They give the title of Ahmad [Mohammed] to Bū Musaylim. . . .

The wine of God, its seal [last result] is pure musk, [but] as for [the other] wine, its seal is stench and torment.[22]

There is a mystery in the way man chooses a master and a spiritual path, which is alluded to by Rūmī himself and which cannot be solved by rational analysis alone. The problem is, how can a candidate for initiation who does not as yet possess spiritual vision distinguish a true master from a false one when there must already be a true master to actualize the possibilities within the disciple and to enable him to distinguish the wheat from the chaff? Herein lies that mysterious relationship between the Spirit and its earthly embodiments that escapes discursive understanding. Man believes that he chooses the way, but in reality he is chosen by the way. What man can do is to pray to find a true master and have reliance upon God while searching. He can, moreover, apply the universal criteria of authenticity and orthodoxy at a time when there are many more

---

[21] This is a direct reference to the act of initiation through which a disciple becomes attached to a particular master and order.

[22] R. A. Nicholson, *The Mathnawī of Jalālu'ddīn Rūmi* (London, 1926), vol. 2, pp. 20–21, with a small alteration in the verse "They make a woolen garb," which Nicholson, basing himself on another version of the original Persian verse, has translated "They make a woolen lion." See also S. H. Nasr, *Sufi Essays*, p. 61 ff.

pretenders than when Rūmī wrote about them, at a time which Christ referred to in his initiatory saying "Many are called but few are chosen."

The Truth has a way of protecting itself from profanation, but the soul of man *can* be destroyed if molded in the hands of someone who does not possess the right qualifications and who is no more than a pretender. Better to remain an agnostic or materialist than to become a follower of some pseudo-spiritual movement that cannot but do harm to what is most precious within man. The Sufis compare man to an egg that must be placed under a hen for a specific period in order to hatch. If, however, it is placed beneath a hen that abandons the egg too soon or does not take sufficient care of it, the egg will never hatch and cannot even be eaten. It will become useless and can only be thrown away. This parable depicts the danger of placing oneself in the hands of a pretender, in the care of those who brush aside centuries of tradition for a supposedly higher and more "evolved" form of spirituality or who want to crash the gates of heaven by means of Sufism without the grace and aid of the Prophet of Islam, whose spiritual presence (*barakah*) alone can enable the initiate to rise upon the ladder of perfection extending to Heaven. We live in dangerous times when the possibilities of error are many, but also, as compensation, when the paths toward God are opened before men in ways never dreamed of before. It remains for each individual to practice discernment and to distinguish between the true and the false, between the way of God and the way of Satan, who is traditionally known as the "ape of God."

Despite all the false masters and forms of pseudo-spirituality, there are still authentic Sufi masters, and the possibility of practicing Sufism in the West is certainly present. But we believe that such a possibility will concern only a few of the vast number of people interested in Sufism today. Most likely, in the near future Sufism will exercise its influence in the West not on one but on three different levels. First of all there is the possibility of practicing Sufism in an active way. Such a path is naturally meant for the few. It demands of man complete surrender to the discipline of the way. To practice it one must follow the famous saying of the Prophet, "Die before you die." One must die to oneself and be reborn spiritually here and now. One must devote oneself to meditation and invocation, to inner purification, to the examining of one's conscience, and to many other practices prevalent among those who actually walk upon the Path (*sālikūn*). There are already some who practice Sufism seriously in the West, and besides the pseudo-Sufi movements of little import, certain branches of Sufism have already sunk their roots in the West and have established authentic branches there. This group is surely bound to grow, although it cannot embrace all those in the West who are now attracted to Sufism.

The second level on which Sufism is likely to influence the West is by presenting Islam in a more appealing form to many who would find in Islamic practices what they are seeking today in the name of Sufism. Because of a long historical background of conflict with the West, Islam has been treated in the Occident until quite recently in the most adverse manner possible. Many who would find exactly what they are looking for in the daily prayers and the fasting of Islam, in its integration of the secular into the sacred, in its dissemination of the sacerdotal function among all men, and in its arts and sciences are driven away because of the manner in which it is usually presented to them. Sufism could help explain Islam by elucidating its most universal and hence in a sense most comprehensible aspect and therefore making it more approachable to outsiders. Usually when people want to study Hinduism they begin with the *Bhagavad-Gita* and not the Law of Manu, whereas in the case of Islam, as already stated, the legalistic aspects are usually taught first and the most universal teachings, if touched upon at all, follow in a disjunctive manner only. As it becomes more fully realized that Sufism is an integral part of Islam and the flower of this tree of revelation, the possibility of the practice of Islam for many who are now attracted to Sufism but who cannot undertake the difficult disciplines of the Path itself will become more evident.

There is no question here of proselytizing, but the fact remains that many in the West are seeking Oriental religious forms to practice and follow in their everyday lives but put Islam aside because they do not identify it with its spiritual aspect, of which Sufism is the essence. Once this identification is clearly made, Sufism may play a role in the West similar to the role it played in India, Indonesia, and West Africa in spreading Islam itself. Of course, in the West its method and extent of activity will certainly be different from what we find in the above instances, but its function will be similar. It will open a possibility within Islam for many earnest Western seekers attracted to Sufism today, and it can also make available to them that intermediate region between esotericism and exotericism which is known to those who have studied the structure of Islam carefully.

Finally, there is a third level upon which Sufism can play an important role in the West, and that is as an aid to recollection and reawakening. Because Sufism is a living tradition with a vast treasury of metaphysical and cosmological doctrines, a sacred psychology and psychotherapy hardly ever studied in the West, a doctrine of sacred art and traditional sciences, it can bring back to life many aspects of the Western tradition forgotten today. Until recently the usual historical works in Western languages on Islam relegated Sufism, along with other aspects of Islamic intellectuality, to the thirteenth century and described it as if it had died long ago. Now, as more people in the West discover that it is a living tradition, contact with its riches can certainly play the role of reawakening Western man to many of his own forgotten treasures. The trends of the past two decades have not been hopeful, but the possibility is nevertheless present.

Moreover, Sufism possesses teachings concerning the nature of man and the world about him that contain keys to the solutions of the most acute problems of the modern world, such as the ecological crisis.[23] Its teachings, if conveyed in a contemporary language, could help solve many present-day problems that have come into being in the first place because of the forgetting of first principles. Its very presence could create through a kind of "sympathetic vibration" the revival of a more authentic intellectual activity and the re-vivification of precious aspects of the Western tradition covered by the dust of the storm created in the period that, paradoxically enough, has come to be known as the Renaissance.

If, however, Sufism is to provide some of the present-day needs of the West it must be able to preserve its own integrity and purity. It must be able to resist the powerful forces of deviation, distortion, and dilution visible everywhere today. It must serve the world about it like a crystal that gathers the light and disseminates it to its surroundings. At the same time it must be able to address the world around it in a language that world understands. Sufism cannot leave the voice of those who call upon it unanswered. Nor can it in any way compromise its principles in order to become more fashionable or widely heard, to become a fad that would disappear from the

[23] See S. H. Nasr, *The Encounter of Man and Nature; the Spiritual Crisis of Modern Man*, chapter 3.

scene with the same rapidity with which it had become popular.

In order to present Sufism in a serious manner above and beyond transient fads and fancies, it is therefore necessary to remain strictly traditional and orthodox from the point of view of the Sufi tradition and at the same time intelligible to Western man with the particular mental habits he has acquired and the reactions toward things he has developed within himself. Also, in order really to accept and practice the teachings of Sufism it is necessary for the modern aspirant to realize that he is actually drowning and that sacred tradition is a rope, thrown toward him by the Divine Mercy, with which he can save himself. In the present situation those who are rooted in the Sufi tradition and who can also expound it in a manner that is comprehensible to modern man and addresses his real needs bear a great responsibility upon their shoulders. It is for them to preserve the purity and integrity of the message, yet be able to transmit it to men conditioned by the factors that characterize the modern world. But in performing this task, such men fulfill their highest duty and accomplish the most worthy act of charity, for there is no higher form of charity than the expression of the Truth, which alone can provide for man's deepest and most abiding needs.

QUESTIONS AND ANSWERS

Q: You said a drowning man would reach for a rope if it were offered to him. But it seems to me that, especially for Westerners, the reaching for the rope is done by that part of man which has to die, by the ego, the grasping part of a man that always wishes to have more of something—spiritual progress or whatever.

NASR: This is a very fine and delicate question that you ask. But what you say is not quite so. The need for salvation or deliverance, on whatever level, from going to Heaven to being free from all limitation, is itself a spiritual urge that comes from that immortal spark in us which is in fact the very negation of the ego. That in man which criticizes man and realizes his limitations cannot itself be limited. And one of the miracles of the human state is that we sometimes do recognize our limitations—if we are not too full of ourselves. If we are like the cup that is so full that nothing can be added, then we are like those people who don't even know they are drowning. And so they do not search. That's an ignorance which really has no medicine.

Contemplative Christianity

Dom Aelred Graham

. . .

.

To SAY SOMETHING about Christianity as it has come down
to us from its beginnings, with particular reference to the needs of
today—that is the task before me as I understand it. The phrase
"sacred tradition" is arresting, even solemn, though I'm not sure
how meaningful it is. *Tradition* as an idea suggests no difficulty; the
word comes from the Latin and means what has been or is being
transmitted or handed down. In this sense Christians emphatically
claim that theirs is a traditional religion; but how far the Church of
today faithfully represents the original community of believers who
gave their allegiance to Jesus of Nazareth is a perplexing question. It
raises a great many issues, some of them perhaps insoluble.

Nor is the concept of "the sacred" without its difficulties. It in-
vites us to enter regions that are hallowed and set apart, to think of
what is consecrated, of people who, unlike their fellows, are dedicated
to some high calling. Such language is significant enough; it evokes
the forms of initiation without which the great world religions could
hardly be identified. But along this path arise also the antitheses
between the sacred and the profane, the holy and the secular, and
with reference to the Divine, the spatial categories of transcendent
and immanent. But these are modes of thought deriving almost
entirely from Western religion—and I wonder whether today, even
for us of the West, the best and simplest thing to say is not, as has
been said, that the only secular thing on earth is the secular heart
of man.

However none of this impairs the validity of the question so
arrestingly proposed by Professor Needleman. He has rightly begun
our inquiry in terms of a quest for a reality that relatively few have
discovered and many would regard as nonexistent, and he has done
so in a way that challenges and excites. As a Californian he finds
himself surrounded by a ferment of interest, a positive search for
the immediacy of religious experience. Where is this to be found?
With the Jesus People and the Pentecostalists, or at points further

East—or West, depending on which way you start? With the Hindus, the Buddhists (including, of course, Zen), the Taoists, the Sufis? All these in various ways have something to offer, it would appear, that the institutional Church does not have. And yet, if I understand him aright, Professor Needleman wisely has his doubts. Has something got lost in the religious shuffle? No need for such derisive characterizations as "cutting spiritual corners," the urge to "instant mysticism": what needs to be faced is that the test of our religious concern is not our readiness to experiment, even to submit to rigorous discipline (many are willing enough to do this), but our general life-style. Admittedly we cannot be content with religion at second hand; yet maybe there is something we can still learn from past ages, something that underlies all the enduring religious traditions. It is the primacy of those gifts of mind and heart, insight and compassion (often denied to the brilliant and clever, even to the fervently "religious"), which, to the degree that they inform a person's way of life, mark him out as in line with what has been taught by the masters of the spiritual life throughout the centuries.

To be more specific: it might be thought that I, coming from the United Kingdom, a land of ancient traditions, brought up in the Catholic faith, a member of the oldest monastic order in the West, could respond with some confidence to Professor Needleman's challenge. But this is not so. One has only to live abroad for a few years to discover how insular, even local, many of the British traditions are; and we are witnessing before our eyes the dissolution of much of the old-time Catholicism. Some form of monasticism may still provide the surest foothold for those wishing to scale the spiritual heights. But organized monasticism in India preceded Christianity by five hundred years or more: and even when Saint Anthony fled to the Egyptian desert at the end of the third century A.D. to become a monk, his action was as much a repudiation as an endorsement of the institutional Church.

Yet the Christian Church still professedly upholds an immensely significant tradition: it cherishes in one of its oldest formulas *verbum Domini traditum vel scriptum,* "the word of the Lord that has come down to us either orally or in the scriptures." But what, after all, is this Christianity that was handed down? The situation is pretty well documented from, say, 150 A.D.; though up to then, and subsequently, the Christian message has been variously interpreted. But what before then? Nobody knows for sure—and that is one of the factors accounting for the confusion in the Church today. Because Christianity—unlike Hinduism or Mahayana Buddhism—claims to be a religion rooted in history, in what actually happened on this earth, it stands or falls by the person and message of Jesus of Nazareth as he lived and died in early-first-century Palestine. Who was this Jesus?

Many churchmen will still answer the question by citing the official creeds or examining the Bible in the light of those creeds. That will hardly do today. We now know, as certainly as such matters can be known, that the four gospels draw upon earlier sources. They present Jesus as faithfully as their several authors knew how, but with a variety of readers and some underlying theological purpose in mind. The evangelists were concerned, not merely to tell it as it was—this they could hardly know—but also to meet the inquiries, the needs and aspirations, of the believing communities among which the gospels circulated. Thus it is not too extravagant a question to ask, Would those who encountered Jesus as he actually operated in Galilee and Judea, supposing them to be alive today, recognize him more clearly as portrayed in the Fourth Gospel than (allowing for the very different medium) in *Jesus Christ Superstar?*

Then Saint Paul appears on the scene. With him emerges the question, arising from our earliest sources and still not satisfactorily answered, What is Christianity? The headquarters of the primitive Church was at Jerusalem—and so it remained until that city was destroyed by the Romans in the year 70 A.D. Included in the destruction was the disappearance of whatever written records existed of the Jerusalem Church; but that it did not accept at his own valuation the message of Paul can be gathered from the New Testament evidence. The members of the early Jerusalem community regarded Jesus, whom they had personally known, as a crucified prophet. They believed that he had risen from the dead, thereby establishing his Messiahship, and that he would shortly appear again as the Son of Man to destroy the Roman tyranny and establish forever the Kingdom of God.

Saint Paul went further than this: he attached to the crucifixion a saving value that extended to Gentiles as well as Jews. His vision was of the resurrected Christ who made possible a new mode of existence for all men. Paul would have had everyone enjoy his own ecstatic experience of the risen Jesus. In his attempts to bring this about he preached a message in a way that would be acceptable not only to Jews—it was unwelcome, even repugnant, to many of them—but to those already influenced by the current religious philosophies of the Graeco-Roman world.

To take an outstanding example: one of Paul's chief themes is known as the "mystical body of Christ," of which all believers are members. This has affinities with the Stoic philosophy of which Seneca, a contemporary of Paul, was a notable representative. Seneca lays emphasis on the relationship that exists between all human beings. We should not aim at self-sufficiency, as many of the Stoics did, but at helping others and forgiving those who have injured us. We live best when we live for others. He stresses the need for active benevolence. "Nature itself bids me be of use to men," he says, "whether they are slave or free, freed men or free born. Wherever there is a human being there is room for benevolence." And again: "See that you are beloved by all while you live and regretted when you die" (*De Vita Beata*, 24, 3).

By assimilating in part such philosophies as a revived Pythagoreanism and Neo-Platonism, Christian thinkers gave depth to the Church's teaching and articulated a doctrine of spiritual inwardness. But if an esoteric spiritual tradition was kept alive within the Church, the demands of popular religion were fully met. Christians were instructed in a definite belief system by means of a "rule of faith" propounded by the ecclesiastical hierarchy; the pagan "mysteries" were replaced by a Christian liturgy and a series of grace-bestowing sacraments. From its early beginnings the life of the Church was extrovert, outward looking—first, to the coming of the Kingdom, then, progressively, to adjusting its relations with the Roman Empire, to meeting persecution, to organizing its own methods of government, to conducting its ritual, to converting the heathen, to dealing with heresies, to political maneuvering as an established religion; and, today, to interdenominational dialogue.

Could it be that Christianity has now exhausted the possibilities of corporate extroversion, and that the Church's chief need is to turn inward? It is the institutionalized, outward-looking Church that is in danger of falling apart today. Is its "sacred tradition"—to use the phrase—again being manifested among the Jesus People and the Pentecostalists? In part, perhaps: and all honor to the genuine religious content there. But they, like all devotees, must surely beware of the dangers of elitism, the illusion that somehow they are chosen spirits not quite like the rest of us. Transient emotional euphoria is a poor guide to the heart of religion. Furthermore, I would think that any revival of biblical fundamentalism is to promote a retrogade Christianity. Paradoxically, the need today, I suggest, is not to focus on what is distinctively Christian: salvation history, theories of redemption, conventional orthodoxies—but to show how Christianity manifests through history, as emerging in space and time, a religion that is eternal.

Perhaps we can best do this by considering briefly, though in some depth, not so much religion *about* Jesus but the religion *of* Jesus. He is reported to have pointed to what this was in the biblical language familiar to his hearers: they were to love God with all their heart, soul, mind, and strength (Mark 12:30)—that is to say, in modern terminology, they were to identify totally with God, and similarly, through God-dedication, with their neighbor (Mark 12: 31). Taken separately, these requirements are to be found in pre-Christian Judaism (Deuteronomy 6:4; Leviticus 19:18); though Jesus may have been the first to link them explicitly together. At any rate they bring us to the roots of all the higher religions. From these roots have sprung flowers that may differ from one another in appearance but whose nature is the same. Four fundamental doctrines, neatly summarized by Aldous Huxley, underlie the religions of the East:

> First: the phenomenal world of matter and of individualized consciousness—the world of things and animals and men and even gods—is the manifestation of a Divine Ground within which all partial realities have their being, and apart from which they would be nonexistent.
>
> Second: human beings are capable not merely of knowing *about* the Divine Ground by inference; they can also realize its existence by a direct intuition, superior to discursive reasoning. This immediate knowledge unites the knower with that which is known.
>
> Third: man possesses a double nature, a phenomenal ego and an eternal self, which is the inner man, the spirit, the spark of divinity within the soul. It is possible for man, if he so desires, to identify himself with the spirit and therefore with the Divine Ground, which is of the same or like nature with the spirit.
>
> Fourth: man's life on earth has only one end and purpose: to identify himself with the eternal self and so come to the knowledge of the Divine Ground.[1]

[1] Aldous Huxley, Introduction, *Bhagavad-Gita*, trans. by Swami Prabhavananda and Christopher Isherwood (New York, 1944).

Hints of these very doctrines can be discovered, at least in embryo, in the earliest Christian writings as their authors sought acceptance in the Hellenistic world. First: we find Saint Paul making the point to the community of believers at Corinth: "We look not to the things that are seen but to the things that are unseen; for the things that are seen are transient, but the things that are unseen are eternal" (2 Corinthians 4:18). Second: not only Jesus, conceived as God's incarnate Word, must be known, but God himself: "And this is eternal life, that they know thee the only true God . . ." (John 17:3). Third: the phenomenal ego must yield to the eternal self: "For whoever would save his life will lose it; and whoever loses his life for my sake and the gospel's will save it" (Mark 8:35). Experientially, Saint Paul implies, God's spirit testifies to our spirit that we are his children (Romans 8:35). And in a later New Testament document we find the hope expressed that "you may escape from the corruption that is in the world because of passion, and become partakers of the divine nature" (2 Peter 1:4). Fourth: finally, the great eschatological climax: that God may be all in all, "everything to every one " (1 Corinthians 15:28).

Something must now be said more specifically about the possibilities of direct religious experience within the Christian tradition. "Mysticism" is the term often employed in this context to describe what cannot really be described, but I shall use the word more customary in the West, at least among Catholic spiritual writers—"contemplation." I shall try to illuminate our theme with some slight reference to the Eastern as well as the Western tradition.

If we look up the words "contemplation" or "contemplate" in a modern dictionary, we find the meaning given as "to view or consider with continued attention." What is implied here is that there is some object of our contemplation. Saint Thomas Aquinas, for one, would not disagree: for him contemplation is an act of the intellect, though it has its roots in man's affectivity. He thinks of it, of course, as being God-directed. Moreover, for Thomas, those who are called contemplatives devote their whole lives to their objective. Their life-style involves self-discipline—particularly, he thinks (following the monastic tradition), abstention from sexual intercourse—and it is largely made up of reading the scriptures, meditation, and prayer. None of this has been outmoded today. But a lot of water has flowed under the theological and philosophical bridges since the thirteenth century, and we must take account of it if we are to discuss the matter in terms that make sense to our contemporaries.

Was Aquinas, following in the footsteps of Plato and Aristotle, too intellectualist about it all? Underlying his thought, as I understand it, is the effort to make God *real* to ourselves—or better, so to dispose ourselves that God becomes consciously the greatest reality for us. And here we get beyond any faculty psychology—intellect and will and so on—to the involvement of the whole personality. Thus we may rephrase "contemplation of God" (I leave aside the question of "faith" for the moment) as "God-realization": the true contemplative is the God-realized person, or at least one who is on the way to that state. And here we find ourselves, I think, in harmony with the thought both of traditional Hinduism—for which "realization" is the perfect state—and of certain Christian existentialists (Gabriel Marcel, Louis Lavelle) of today.

In Indian thought, it is worth mentioning, God-realization takes place according to the variety of people's temperaments. One person may be inclined to a life of devotion—pouring him/herself out in acts of adoration, prostrations before the Godhead or one of its manifestations, given over to interior aspirations, vocal prayers, some meaningful ritual or liturgy. Another person may give him/herself selflessly to active good works, a concern for the betterment of society, relief of the needy or destitute, trying to bring about, or move a little nearer to, one world instead of our present three. Finally, a third person may be concerned with God-realization in its most direct form: by a deepening awareness, an expansion of consciousness, trying to achieve, or disposing him/herself to, the highest degree of insight and compassion: so that, in Christian terms, "it is no longer I who live, but Christ who lives in me" (Galatians 2:20).

Any one of these three ways, if practiced selflessly, can bring about God-realization. They are not mutually exclusive—it is often a question of emphasis—and they can overlap; but there are good grounds for distinguishing between them. Each, needless to say, has its pitfalls and dangers. The way of devotion can lapse into mere routine, an obsessive piety, a mechanical, even superstitious, carry-out of a set program of observance. The way of active good works can degenerate into mere busy-ness, and at worst, a thrust for power, an itch to organize other people's lives. The way of deepening awareness can dissolve into an ego-trip, a quest for self-satisfaction, and an indifference to our neighbor's problems and difficulties. But I think that the masters of the spiritual life, both East and West, would agree that these risks have to be taken—and particularly the risks attending the most worth-while objective—what Buddhists call "seeing into one's own nature"—since the wisdom that ensues is the most effective source of any fruitful activity.

The reason that the concept of "realization" seems to me preferable to "contemplation" is that the latter suggests a subject-object relationship: a knowing subject over against a known object. But God can never be a known object—a fact that may be concealed by the rather misleading metaphor "the vision of God" with which Christians sometimes describe eternal happiness. Aquinas is aware of the difficulty here. According to his theory of knowledge, what we know must be conceptualized by our minds; but no finite concept can embrace God; therefore the divine Logos itself must play the role of concept. And when we couple with this the point that the Source of our being (that is, the Godhead) is more inward to us than we are to ourselves, then in this case any opposition between subject and object is broken down as effectively as it is, say, in Martin Buber or Nikolai Berdyaev.

Let us glance for a moment at Buber. He is a great exponent of what is involved in person-to-person relations. "Being true to the being in which and before which I am placed," he says, "is the one thing that is needful."[2] According to Buber, as is well known, there are two primary attitudes we may bring to the world, and these attitudes express themselves in two primary words, or rather, combination of words: "I-It" and "I-Thou." There is no "I" taken in itself, apart from combination with "It" or "Thou." The primary word "I-It" can never be spoken with the whole being. The "I-Thou" relation is described as "meeting" or "encounter." It is a relation not of subject to object but of subject to subject. The various "Thous" with which we come into relation may be thought of as constituting a perspective, the extended lines of which meet in the eternal "Thou," or God. Every particular "Thou" is a glimpse through to the eternal "Thou."

When it comes to communicating with the eternal "Thou," the ultimate reality we call God, we are at the same time concerned with our own deepest self. Not our superficial empirical ego, which we are all too ready to distinguish from every other ego, but the ground of our being in which all humanity is kin, of which we are always at least implicitly aware but which can never be the object of direct conceptual knowledge. "Let me know myself," says Saint Augustine; "let me know Thee." Martin Heidegger makes the same point in existentialist terms: "The question of God and the question of myself are identical." A similar point is made by Nikolai Berdyaev, though in rather a different way. He takes the view that, whatever is to be said of the material objects with which the physical sciences deal, spiritual reality is, so to speak, behind us in the life of the subject rather than spread out before us in the objective world. "There is no greater mistake," says Berdyaev "than to confuse objectivity and reality. The objective is that which is least real."

Contemplation, we don't need to be told, is not to concentrate on what is "up there," but to *realize*—that is, make real to ourselves— what is most inward, the very ground of our being—or to put it less inaccurately, Being itself: considered not as an entity, or an essence, but dynamically as *existence*. Paul Tillich, I believe, is correct in affirming that to say that "God is being itself" is the only univocal statement that can be made about God. "After this has been said nothing else can be said about God as God which is not symbolic." Not that this is to belittle in any way symbolic language; it is the language of all poetry and it often speaks to us with a significance unattainable by a more literal use of terms. We should note, however, that no religious symbol may be treated as an absolute, since that would be to turn it into an idol.

All initiatives clearly lie with Being itself. And here is where, on our part, both grace and faith come in. Those who take the view that ultimate reality, assuming that it exists, is indifferent or mean-ingless, will, like Jean-Paul Sartre or Albert Camus, quite consistently be atheists. But here I would like to refer to Professor Needleman's significant encounter with Greek Orthodoxy in the person of the Abbot of Stavroniketa. "One must *begin* with faith," said Father Vassilios. How true! But behind faith in some avatar or incarnation of the Divine must lie the basic trust that the ultimately Existent is more creative than destructive, that the power behind the universe is not neutral but gracious, beneficent. That, I think, beyond the creeds and protestations of one or another orthodoxy, is what re-ligious faith fundamentally is.

If we are sufficiently responsive, Being itself grasps us and manifests itself to us in what the sacred traditions regard as revelation. Human reason is not at this point overwhelmed; rather, in what we have been calling "realization," reason is raised to·an ecstatic level on which the seeming opposition of subject and object is overcome and there results an experience of the Divine. And here we may add that to experience God is to experience the true self—the self that we find when we have forgotten about our ego. To the Christian understanding (and here again I am persuaded by Tillich), Jesus as the particular manifestation of the Divine became the Christ, the "new being." The new being is the power beyond man's normal consciousness that heals his existential conflicts and overcomes his sin—sin being understood as his estrangement from himself, from others, and from the ground of his being. "Putting on Christ"—to use the Pauline phrase (Galatians 3:27)—means that we ourselves share in the new being which Christ is. None of this takes place in isolation. Gabriel Marcel sees a chain of four notions, successive but overlapping, that indicate the movement toward realization. They are: person, engagement, community, reality. In other words, only by engaging ourselves in community can we reach reality.

But let us look, briefly though a little more closely, at some of the demands that, according to the traditions of both East and West, the contemplative state, or the call to realization, has to meet. This brings us back to the way of discipline usefully summarized by Saint Thomas as *lectio, meditatio, oratio.* The first, *lectio,* is self-explanatory: to take some familiar or appealing text of Scripture, should we feel the need for it, as a starting point for concentrating the mind. Meditation is perhaps a little more complicated. The Western Christian tradition generally indicates that meditation should be *about* something—and that something can often be quite detailed and specific, at least for those influenced by the post-Reformation technique of Saint Ignatius Loyola, with its composition of place and the exercise of the visual imagination. The Eastern tradition, on the other hand, corresponds somewhat to the medieval Catholic approach—as this stems from pseudo-Denis the Areopagite, is later represented by Meister Eckhart and the anonymous author of *The Cloud of Unknowing,* and might be said to culminate in certain experiences of Saint John of the Cross. It is here, I think, that meditation merges into contemplation. At this point is reached the ground of being, a cognitive experience whose content cannot be verbalized, except perhaps in poetic symbols. The various sacred traditions describe it according to their own characteristic belief systems, but what they refer to is, I think, the same in each.

"Those who perform meditation for even one session," writes the Zen Master Hakuin, "destroy innumerable accumulated sins." As is well known, the Hindu-Buddhist tradition holds that sitting, and sitting in a certain way, is the best posture for meditating. (*The Cloud* also refers to sitting meditation—what Japanese Buddhists call *zazen*). Here is a famous Zen text (from the Sixth Patriarch, Hui-nêng) which shows that the phrase "sitting meditation" can also be used metaphorically. "Outwardly to be in the world of good and evil yet with no thought arising in the heart, this is sitting (*za*)." "Inwardly to see into one's own nature and not move from it, that is meditation (*zen*)."

"With no thought arising in the heart"—there is the paradox, to be found also as the culminating point of Hindu Yoga: the "cessation of the movements of the mind." At a certain stage we are helped by thinking about God, or what we might suppose is God; but thoughts and words about God can become obstacles as well as helps. They are always in some degree untrue. "Why do you prate about God? Whatever you say about him is false," said Eckhart, using the outspoken language that got him into trouble with the ecclesiastics. However that may be, at least we find agreement among the masters in teaching that we dispose ourselves most effectively to God's self-revelatory action by living in the present on the spot where we are—that is to say, not daydreaming hopefully about the future or nostalgically about the past, but harboring no illusions. Just *being* rather than *having*, as Marcel expresses it.

All the great religious traditions, besides their rituals and often elaborate symbology, advocate the use of *mantras*—short, pregnant phrases, often vocalized, whose purpose is to focus the mind, to eliminate distractions. Well known to Christians is the Jesus prayer from the *Philokalia* of the Greek Orthodox Church—in its full form, "Lord Jesus Christ, Son of God, have mercy on me," though it is often contracted to just one or two words. The practice of it is attractively described in that moving, anonymously written little book *The Way of a Pilgrim*. We can, of course, make up mantras for ourselves. Thus, *The Cloud* advocates the repetition over and over of just one word—"God" or "Jesus," which can easily be turned into the invocation "God be praised."

Eastern religions have, as is well known, their earlier equivalents to all this—for example, the most sacred of the Hindu mantras, *Aum*; or the popular *Hari Krishna*, which can often be heard chanted processionally along the public streets of our big cities. Then again the *Nembutsu* of Japanese Buddhists, or the famous Tibetan mantra *Om mani padme hum*, which is chanted today in Buddhist monasteries in Nepal, Sikkim, and Bhutan. Gandhi, it may be remembered, uttered the Hindu mantra *Hē Rama* after being fatally shot.

But where, finally, does all this lead to? Perhaps to that state, as mentioned in the *Philokalia*, "above which there is nothing to wish for and beyond which there is nowhere to go"? Nothing to wish for, nowhere to go—could that be the key we are looking for? Among modern Western thinkers Martin Heidegger seems to me nearest the heart of the matter. He calls for an attitude of mind that penetrates beyond entities, singular or collective, a kind of thinking that is submissive to being itself. Heidegger holds that most Christians think of their God as an entity, and therefore go astray—in which judgment he is unfair, at least to the medieval Catholicism of Saint Thomas and *The Cloud*. But the point needs to be emphasized that the contemplative mind must get beyond all entities and particularities and be prepared to face the *void*—which is by no means pure negation (as is often thought), merely no-thing-ness. The "nothingness," the existential *angst* of which Heidegger speaks, is the anxiety or malaise (what the Zen people call the "great doubt") that occurs when the entire world of entities sinks into undifferentiated meaninglessness. Perhaps this is but a facet of Saint John of the Cross's "void," the Buddhist "emptiness," which transcends the opposition between meaningless and meaningful (since *meaning* always implies a reference elsewhere). Only when one faces this, and includes in it the prospect of one's own inevitable death, can one reach the unshakable joy and equanimity that comes from the contemplation, or realization, of being—"such sober certainty of waking bliss."

God is never to be known directly, only through some form of his self-manifestation. The metaphor of "the vision of God," therefore, should not suggest to our minds a positive flash of insight. What is indicated is the condition in which we regard our cognitive powers as a kind of clearing in being, when, through the deepest self-awareness, we become the *locus* where being is lit up and becomes unconcealed—remembering that unconcealedness is the equivalent of truth, in the primordial sense of *aletheia*.

Let us bring this line of thought a little closer to expressing the God of traditional Christianity, and we might add, to the ultimate reality of Hinduism. Consider the doctrine of the Holy Trinity: to the Father can be appropriated the source of all being; to the Son, the Logos, belongs infinite consciousness; to the Spirit pertains the joy that flows from love without limit. "To be," "to know," "to find joy" correspond to the *sat, cit, ananda*—the Being, Consciousness, Bliss—of the *Upanishads*. This doctrine is echoed without variation, though in existential terms, in one of the aphorisms of Saint John of the Cross: "In order to be All, do not desire to be anything. In order to know All, do not desire to know anything. In order to find the joy of All, do not desire to enjoy anything."

Let me conclude with the observation that our religious "experience" is of small account to anyone but ourselves. Only that of which it is the by-product can in some degree be transmitted. Christianity's one authentic message is to proclaim that God and our neighbor be loved—utterly. Transposed into Buddhist terms, may we not say, take care of wisdom and compassion, and *nirvana* will look after itself? The genetic code indicates that we are heirs of the ages, traditionalists despite ourselves. Facing reality with all the mental clarity and honesty we can achieve, dynamically accepting and responding—that is what a life that makes sense is about. And for some reason we cannot quite understand, it appears that this is the only way to happiness.

QUESTIONS AND ANSWERS

Q: *It seems to me that a life devoted to contemplation and meditation would not leave much energy for being worldly. That is, someone who followed this path would probably not be the person to whom you would take your car when it broke down. I mention this because when people are growing up they have to face a fairly complicated world. Is it possible to live by concentrating only on spiritual essentials and being ignorant of technology, the stock market, how to make a living, and so on? How should energies be divided between these different kinds of demands?*

GRAHAM: Well to the point. I have been stressing the deeper things of the spiritual life, particularly meditation, because I think a large number of people today are interested in that. But I tried to make it clear that there are at least three ways that can lead to God-realization. We find these ways present not only in Christianity but in many other traditions as well. For some people it is the adoration of God through personal worship, church-going, and participation in the liturgy that leads to God-realization; for others it is meditation and contemplation. But there is also a way of action, of selfless service to others in the context of ordinary life. Anyone who can work in the world for the betterment of human life can also become a God-realized person.

Q: Is some form of asceticism necessary?

GRAHAM: Well, as you probably know, asceticism is the same word as athleticism and means some kind of practice, some kind of discipline, some kind of controlling of one's bodily and mental powers. But that discipline, in itself, is to some degree a condition of spiritual well-being. Unless this is remembered, asceticism easily becomes overstressed. I think the best form of asceticism is in the service of other people. If we are sufficiently concerned with what is in us and around us we do not have to look for any special means of making life inconvenient for ourselves.

Q: Why do you suppose that the wish for something higher is limited to so few?

GRAHAM: I wonder how true that is. The term "higher" is a spatial metaphor that can be very misleading. Though it's true, I think, that many people do not have very conscious spiritual aspirations, nevertheless I think that most people are dissatisfied with themselves in one way or another. They feel that they are not always their own true selves, that they have a greater potential than is being realized. And that is what I mean by spiritual aspirations—not taking flight into the heavenly sphere, if indeed there is one.

Q: What place does the maxim "know thyself" have in Christianity as you understand it? And if it does have a place, could you say something about the effort that must be made?

GRAHAM: I think, perhaps, that your question implies that the "know thyself" doctrine is not fully developed in Christianity, and that this lack is one of the problems with the Church today. Certainly, Saint Augustine speaks of "let me know myself, let me know thee," and he was very anxious to know his own true self. But then he had a very splendid but rather chaotic mind and got himself involved in a whole lot of other questions and tended to forget about himself.

Q: The psychedelics have raised many questions about the experience of emptiness and changes in consciousness. Do you feel these drugs can be spiritually useful?

GRAHAM: I have good reason to believe that changes of consciousness can take place by the use of drugs and by the ingesting of certain vegetables. Certainly some insight can occur, but I think that most people who have had those experiences, and who have felt a new level of psychological content would admit that this objective can be achieved more effectively without the use of drugs. It seems to me highly understandable and very human that young people would like to experiment a little with drugs, to try everything once. But from my own experience I would have to say that it is highly doubtful that anything permanently new could come from that quarter, especially in relation to a long-term life-style that could bring one closer to God.

Q: How is the knowledge or contemplation of God linked with the transformation of man—the attainment of his complete potentiality?

GRAHAM: Since all initiative comes from being itself—that is to say, from the Godhead—it is probably impossible to know how far man can develop. To become like Christ or the Buddha seems to me to depend more on the grace of God, the giving of God, than on the efforts of our individual egos. In any case, this kind of perfection can only be realized by degrees within each person.

Q: If one seeks the void or the no-thing, what is the position of Jesus in this search?

GRAHAM: I suggested once in print somewhere, and nobody wrote to the journal to complain about it, that Jesus in his passion experienced the void. Of course, the whole of Jesus' language about God is the traditional Jewish language. He constantly uses human terms, anthropomorphic phraseology, to talk about God. Even in the garden of Gethsemane in his agony he says, "Father if it be possible, let this chalice pass from me." So he still thinks of God in positive terms—as Father. But on the cross he says, "My God, my God, why hast thou deserted me?" It is "my God" that has deserted him, the God he has always thought about in his human mind. That God has vanished, leaving only the void.

Myth, Symbol, and Tradition

P. L. Travers

. . .

.

IN SPEAKING OF the traditions, I speak not as an anthropologist or a doctor of divinity or a historian of comparative religion—nothing as grand as any of these—but simply as a storyteller. My way of approaching the traditions is a storyteller's way—through the myth, legend, folklore, and indeed the fairy tale to which they are so inextricably bound.

Anything I have to say, therefore, will come from the same storehouse as those chronicles we refer to, always pejoratively, I'm afraid, as Old Wives' tales and Superstition.

But can we, I wonder, dismiss these lightly? What, after all, is superstition? If we examine it at its root we will find that the word comes from *super stitia*—that which stands over; therefore, by extension, that which remains, the last tail-end of something that has in the past had truth and meaning; a part that has by chance escaped the holocaust of time and which, since it is only a part, is inevitably misunderstood and very often reviled as meaningless. But may there not be a positive side to superstition? Perhaps if we could grasp that tail and patiently let it draw us backward, we might come upon the main body, its very head and source.

As to Old Wives, we do wrong to ignore our debt to them. I speak feelingly because, being a storyteller, I am inevitably something of an Old Wife myself! And who else, other than Old Wives, has preserved for us all the myth and folklore, all the fairy tales, and all the legends that are wound about the great traditions as thread is wound round a spindle; those records that, far from being out of date and unscientific, are the true facts of that inner world, unseen but nearer than a man's neck vein, that interpenetrates our lives at every level and fructifies our dreams.

You will realize, of course, that here I am speaking figuratively, that Old Wives in this connection are not just a bunch of gray-haired grandmothers spinning stories in rocking chairs, but all the chroniclers from the beginning of time—named or unnamed, it doesn't matter—who have handed down by word or pen the annals

of man's inner life. You will find their footprints everywhere, even—
or perhaps I should say particularly—in the minuscule world of childhood, where even the games and nursery rhymes come straight out
of myth and tradition.

Take as an example the old song "London Bridge Is Falling
Down." This singing game, often known nowadays as "Oranges and
Lemons," was played and sung under one name or another before
London ever existed. Sometimes it was known as "Angels and Devils"; in France it is still called "Heaven and Hell" and in Germany
"Sun and Moon," but always it concerns a bridge. For our ancient
forefathers, as the Old Wives tell us, attached great importance—a
spiritual importance—to bridges. The Devil, it seems—or to put it
more mythologically, the elemental spirit of the land who detests
any interference with the natural world and prefers to divide rather
than to connect—had a strong aversion to bridges. His repeated
efforts to bring them to ruin called for substantial placatory offerings, even at times human sacrifice. For it was widely believed that
the soul, when separated from the body, had to cross a bridge on
its perilous journey from one world to the next. At all costs, therefore, London Bridge—build it up with stone so strong!—and all
other bridges had to be kept in existence lest the soul should fall
into enemy hands on its way toward the angel. So you see how even
a children's game can lead us back, by its single thread, into a world
of meaning.

And what of that old nursery riddle, "How Many Miles to Babylon?" Why Babylon, one has to ask, a city dead for thousands of
years, and why should we want to go there? But when one remembers that the word Babylon means "the gate of God," the following
line, "Three score and ten"—the biblical span of a man's life—seems
the only possible answer. A lifetime to get to Babylon! Three score
years and ten to get to the gate of God. You see what the riddle
is telling us. You see how Mother Goose lifts her wings and carries
us back to antiquity!

These and their like are indeed tail-ends, but tail-ends that are the
residue of a vast and potent body of teaching that once so pervaded
every aspect of life that the smallest child was aware of it.

Does this, then, mean that we have to become as little children
in order to discover it afresh? I think it does, in the sense that we
have to find again in ourselves the child that asked "Why was I
born?" and "What is my meaning?" The questions, of course, are still

there, though silted over by all the triviality of life, all the desacralization. But, paradoxically, that desacralization can, if we examine it, point us a path to the sacred—just as the negative declaration that God is dead is, in fact, a positive assurance that God has at some time been alive. The opposites invoke each other. And "Danger itself," as Hölderlin said, "calls forth the rescuing power." Or, as Mircea Eliade has so rightly put it, "The man who has made his choice in favor of a profane life never succeeds entirely in doing away with religious behavior. Even the most desacralized existence still preserves traces of a religious valorization of the world"; and, further, that "myth and symbol are the very stuff of spiritual life. They may be disguised, mutilated, and depraved but are never extirpated."

It is true. The myths and traditions are in our blood, deny them though we will. After all, though we have largely forgotten that the very word means "Christ's mass," we still celebrate Christmas. The giving of gifts, whether or not we care to remember it, commemorates the gifts of the Wise Men, of gold, frankincense, and myrrh. But our feasting and the decking of a green tree have an even older root. They recall to us our archaic fathers, whose Saturnalia at the winter solstice, the darkest of all times of the year, was a ritual calling back of the sun as a preparation for spring.

As for kissing under the mistletoe at this season, it harkens right back to the time of the Druids for whom the mistletoe was a sacred plant, a plant homologized to the sun. The golden bough, by means of which Aeneas was able to pass through the underworld and return alive to the light of day, was a branch of mistletoe. And it was a sprig of mistletoe, the one plant that had not promised not to harm him, that killed Baldur the Beautiful, the god of light of the Northern myths. It is for all these reasons—to partake of the ancient Druid magic, to pass from darkness into light, and to keep each other from being harmed that we make the placatory gesture.

It is the same with our New Year festivities. All the noise and clamor, the farewells and the greeting, all the making of good resolutions are a reminder of the myth of eternal return, the periodic destruction and re-creation of the cosmos, common not only to primitive but to all religions, when the world and time and man himself, after a ritual pause, were ritually renewed. I only began to think about this ritual pause after I had in fact written a story embodying it. As a mere storyteller perhaps I may be permitted to tell a mere story. There is in one of my books a New Year chapter called "Happy Ever After." A child asks "When does the old year end?" "On the first stroke of midnight," says Mary Poppins. "And the new year—when does it begin?" "On the last stroke of midnight," says Mary Poppins. "Well, what then happens in between while the clock is striking twelve?" Well, what did happen in between? In asking the conundrum the child and, of course, the storyteller had happened upon the ritual pause. In the story the pause is called the Crack. And the Crack is in effect synonymous with the country spoken of in "Rumpelstiltzkin," "where the fox and the hare say good night to each other"—in a word, the country where the opposites are reconciled. Red Riding Hood and the Wolf are friends, the lion and the unicorn cease fighting for the crown, the Sleeping Beauty and the Wicked Fairy lean over and kiss each other. And the Farmer's Wife, for a few brief strokes of the clock, puts away her carving knife and spares the Three Blind Mice. The Crack is, in fact, the place and the time; perhaps—I thought—the only place and the only time when to be Happy Ever After is possible and true. Long after I had written this chapter about the ritual pause I listened to a roving reporter on the radio telling of how he had visited an African tribe at the end of *their* solar year. He described the chanting and the drumming and how at a given moment all this suddenly ceased while the gods invisibly withdrew. For a few moments there was complete silence. Then the drums broke out again in triumph, acclaiming the gods as they returned to rule over another year. "And," added the reporter, "though I do not ask you to believe it, I can vouch for the fact that my tape-recorder, for those few moments of ritual silence, ceased spinning and was still!" Well, as one who has a sort of sneaking respect for superstition, I found that I could believe it. Just as there is in Yoga practice the ritual pause in the held breath between the breathing out and the breathing in. Between one lifetime and the next, between one breath-time and the next, something waits for a moment.

Our profane life is full of these hidden meanings, of clues that we constantly overlook because we do not know what to look for. Brides are still lifted over thresholds for fear that they should stumble. But who knows why? Who remembers that thresholds, whether in human habitations or in temples and churches, were in old times places of significance? The threshold is the frontier between two worlds where sacred and profane at the same moment oppose and communicate with each other, where one world begins and another ends.

To stumble at such a meeting-place would surely be unpropitious; one *needs* to be lifted over.

And marriage itself, while occasionally still a sacrament in what remains of our Christian world, is also a pattern or paradigm of something very much older—the mythical mating of the sky god and the earth goddess and the interaction of Yang and Yin, the male and female principles, from whose meeting, in the words of the *Tao Te-Ching*, come all the ten thousand things. Which means to say everything that exists.

Even house warmings, wholly secular though they now are, hold a faint memory of the poured libations by means of which religious man, in making a place for himself to dwell in—and thereby imitating the act of world-creation—invoked the blessing of the gods.

And what of the mythical structures that underlie the mass media, especially in the United States? Every comic strip presents a modern version of the mythological hero. One has only to think of the popularity of Superman or Batman or Dick Tracy to realize that, far from being dead, myth—though in a degraded form—is still vigorous and alive and actively willed and wished for.

It is the same with the novel and the detective story. The need for the hero and heroine in one and the hero and villain in the other is the age-old need, camouflaged and profane as it is, for mythological worlds and times.

Even the modern reverence for—one might almost say worship of—sport has in it a taste, a flavor, or at any rate the ghost of a flavor, of the Greek and Roman games, the principal purpose of which was "to maintain a sacred energy with which the life of Nature, or of a human group or an important personage" was connected. The games were a ritual, either in salute to the illustrious living or in memory of the illustrious dead, by means of which the world of the gods as well as the worlds of the dead and the living were periodically rejuvenated.

One could go on and on with examples—all the primal stuff that we have forgotten, all the meaning that has been let fall into the subterranean layers of the mind. In order to fish it up we have to become once more aware, as our ancient fathers were well aware, that by the mere fact of having a body, the mere fact of being born, each of us has assumed a place in the universe and is part of all that is. The myths and their attendant symbols can help us to find and understand this place.

It should be recognized here that myth is not used in its contemporary sense of "fiction" or "illusion" but myth as it was originally understood, myth as primordial reality, myth as revelation and precedent, myth as a model to be imitated.

"It is not" as Nietzsche said, "that there is some hidden thought or idea at the bottom of myth, as some people have supposed, but the myth itself is a kind or style of thinking. It imports an idea of the universe in its sequence of events, actions, and sufferings."

That phrase "a kind of thinking" is wonderfully apt, for it is a fact that there are things and events that cannot be described other than mythologically. Not long ago I watched a scientist on television turning himself almost inside out in his effort to find the right words to describe the birth and the death of the universe. At last he said reluctantly, as though ashamed of the unscientific statement, "It is as though it was breathed out and then breathed in again." He did not go so far as to say by whom the breathing was done: it was clear that he had never heard of the myth of the days and nights of Brahma. It arose and spoke itself in him. Science, in its efforts to explain the inexplicable, is always in danger of explaining it away. It has never heard of the Chinese ideogram Pai, which in one context means "explain" and in another "in vain." In vain to explain, how marvelous!

One could also say of myth that as well as showing man his place in the universe, it is designed to make him aware of the fact that he is meant to be something more than his own personal history and, more especially, to place him squarely between the two opposing forces that keep him and the world in balance. For this cosmic dialectic between good and evil, hero and villain, is a major theme of all mythology—the two Earth Shapers, one bounteous, all-giving, and healing; the other producing the diseases and troubles of every kind and order—the benign and the malignant interacting, balancing and checking and disciplining each other to produce a viable world. One has only to think of the Greek myth of Prometheus—forethought—and his brother Epimetheus—afterthought; of Ahura Mazda of the Zoroastrians of Persia, who stands for the power of good over against Angra Mainyu, the power of evil; of Vishnu the preserver and Shiva the destroyer as one finds them in Hindu myth; of the angels and devils of Christianity or of the two heroes of the Navaho Indian myth—Water-Child, the son of the rivers, and Monster-Slayer, born of fire—the life-giving sap of one tempering the solar aspect of the other. And all these pairs, and countless others, can be subsumed under the Chinese symbol of the Great

Ultimate, which Zen has purloined and made its own, the white fish with black eye, black fish with white eye within the encompassing and reconciling circle.

Myths come, it is true, from the ancient past, but it is no less true that they, like the traditions round which they gather, are constantly being rediscovered, renewed, and restated.

One has only to think of the movement for Women's Liberation, whose groundswell is being felt throughout the world, to understand myth in action, myth working in a contemporary setting. Consider. The Great Goddess, mother and origin of all deities, the first to arise and the first to be worshiped, has long been subjugated by the masculine gods—too long, apparently, for her. Now she has had enough of it, she has flung their feet from off her neck and is rising in her wrath. A myth denied is taking its revenge and is now in the process of being resuscitated and relived.

She has waited long, the divine mother. But the myths can afford to abide their time, for ultimately they are timeless. So also, in spite of all that has accrued to them from history, are the traditions. It is impossible to speak of either as having been invented but rather that, in the words of a Zen *koan*, they were not created but summoned.

Carl Gustav Jung has written, "One could almost say that if all the world's traditions were cut off at a single blow, the whole mythology and the whole history of religion would start all over again with the next generation."

What a wonderful statement to have almost made! The traditions, like the myths, exist whether you and I note them or forget them, as the River Ganges is always flowing whether we bathe in it or not. We need no new traditions, only to understand the purport of those we have. And even if the traditions were lost, the very children would refashion them. A young man whom I know well began a story when he was about five with "It happened in the first world." And when I asked tentatively, dreading to break the thread between his words and his inner kingdom, "Tell me, is there a second?" he answered with the utmost assurance and a look of astonishment at my apparent ignorance, "Yes, of course, there are three of them. That one, this, and another." But no one had spoken to him of the three worlds, no one had spoken of the soul; no one had told him that man comes to this world from afar and still has far to go. He knew it without the telling.

It was this same child who invited, or rather required me, to play a part in a drama that he and his friends were enacting. "What is the name of the play?" I asked and was told that it was the story of Finn MacCool. Finn MacCool is one of the great chieftains of Irish legend. "And we need you," he said, "for the Virgin Mary, the mother of Finn MacCool."

My surprise at such a juxtaposition of characters was only momentary, for I realized that in a world where everything is myth it had a kind of logic. Since the Virgin Mary had given birth to one great hero of the world why not, in the child's mind, to an endless race of heroes? D. H. Lawrence, I remembered, had made a distinction between the truth of fact and the truth of truth. The truth of fact is history; it records the dates of kings and battles; but the truth of truth has the whole of mythology for its realm. The child, in this world, was within his rights.

That same truth of truth was at work in a short essay that was recently sent me by a schoolteacher from the pen of one of her younger pupils. "The Lord," it said, "is the father of all things and Mary Poppins is the mother of all things and they are married—or has been married—and they are both a miracle." Well, we, of course, can laugh at this but the pupil was busy with his own mythology, adjusting it to his inner perception and arranging for his own satisfaction that his two favorite characters should together create the world.

I remember, too, the daughter of some friends of mine who, being convinced atheists, had carefully protected their offspring from any virus of religion. One day the child was discovered carefully and cautiously hiding something under a corner of the carpet, and her parents were horrified to find that the object was a small cross made of two sticks tied with string. "But why?" they demanded, in outraged voices. "I love it!" she answered simply, as she slipped the treasure under her pillow for safety. By some means that Jung, perhaps, would have understood when he said that "one must be able to let things happen in the psyche," she had found her way to one of the most ancient of all symbols—far older than Christianity. As children, we know more than we know we know. But even when we have lost what we know—or repressed it into the depths of our being—it is possible for any strong and deep experience to awaken the myths and symbols and align us to a tradition—this one or that, it hardly matters; our psychic need will choose.

For tradition itself is a unitary whole and its separate aspects are, as it were, dialects of one and the same language of the spirit. This is borne out by the similarity, the brotherly likeness that is to be found between the symbols of all traditions. Take, for instance, the Omphalos, the navel of the earth. Every holy place in every tradition is looked upon as a center of the world, a place where the sacred enters the profane, where the immeasurable is reflected back to that which can be measured and the energy of eternity pours itself into time—Mount Olympus, for instance, from which the Greek gods descended to the earth; Mount Meru of the Hindus, Mount Zion and Mount Tabor in Palestine; the Rock of Jerusalem, which was thought to be the navel from which the whole earth originally unfolded; the Field of Golgotha, which is homologized to the Garden of Eden in order that the new Adam could be crucified at the place where the old Adam was created; the Kaaba in Mecca, the sacred spot of the world community of Islam; Borobodur, the great Buddhist navel in Java; the sacred lodge of the Algonquin Indians; the underground kiva of the Hopis. One could go on with this list forever for, as Mircea Eliade has truly said, "The multiplicity or even infinity of centers of the world raises no difficulty for religious thought, concerned as it is not with geometrical or geographical space but with existential and sacred space." Therefore it can be said that for religious man his temple, his cathedral, his church, his dwelling-house, even, indeed, his own body is symbolically situated at the center of the world. For where is the spring, where are the hearth and home of myth, tradition, and symbol? Where else could these be but in man himself? How could they be outside him?

Another symbol common to all traditions and one to which the navel spot can be assimilated is the cosmic axis—that axis which, in whatever form it takes, connects the three worlds—the underworld, earth, and Heaven. Sometimes, as in Dante, it is a mountain whose roots are in the Inferno and whose head is in Paradise. In many traditions it takes the form of a cosmic pillar. One thinks of the famous pillar that the Saxons called Irminsul and which was held by them to support all things and that Charlemagne so irreligiously destroyed; the *skambha*, the cosmic pillar of the Rig Veda, the earliest of the Hindu scriptures; the great Roman pillars, and the obelisks of Egypt. And there are certain Australian tribes that carry with them on their wanderings a sacred pole that supports their world and insures continuous communication with the world of the sky. The spires of Gothic cathedrals and the minarets of Islamic mosques serve the same purpose, so do the ziggurats of Persia. They are all cosmic pillars. Even the Milky Way was in ancient times held to be a path or pillar. And in old British maps, one can find Watling Street, which is still one of the thoroughfares of the city of London, continuing all the way through Europe and ending up in the Milky Way. How graphically the point is made here that there is no discontinuity between one world and another, no break in the path of pilgrim man on his way from earth to Heaven. The pillar-path is everywhere. Among the North American Indians and the Mongolians of Northern Asia it is symbolized by the central post of the human habitation; for the herdsmen of Central Asia the path of the smoke through an opening at the top of the tent—or yurt—serves the same purpose. And one cannot go far in Mexico without coming upon wooden posts set up and notched with many steps by which the shaman, serving as man's intermediary between what is lower and what is higher, can take off on his magical climb from one world to another.

A variant of the cosmic pillar and one that serves the same purpose is the continually recurring symbol of the World Tree. In the ancient Norse and Teutonic myths the universe is supported by the great tree Yggdrasil, which extends from the nether world to the very top of Heaven. One of its roots is grounded in the fountain of Mimir, from whose sacred waters flows all the wisdom of the world. Close to another root dwell the Norns—who are the equivalent of the Greek fates. And at the foot of the third lies the lake of memory and premonition, to achieve which qualities the high god Odin paid the price of one of his eyes. In one of the oldest Norse sagas it is said that "King Volsung let build a noble hall in such wise that a big oak tree stood therein and that the limbs of the tree blossomed fair out over the roof of the hall while below stood the trunk within it and the said tree did men call Branstock." When we remember that that name Branstock is the equivalent of Burning Bush we are brought to the very heart of the symbol. Even today in Germany— and I have seen it also in Switzerland—whenever a new house is built a living tree or a green branch is set up upon the beams at a certain stage as an act of ritual and dedication, creating a world axis in little, a metaphorical Branstock.

Coming to our own tradition, we can think of the cross as the world tree par excellence. There is an old belief, part of our Christian mythology, that the wood from the cross on which Christ was hanged was hewn from one of the trees that grew in Paradise. For Genesis makes a distinction between two world trees—one of the knowledge of good and evil and the other the tree of life. But both trees are specifically said to be in the midst of the garden, therefore at the navel of the earth and one is tempted to ask, with Ananda Coomaraswamy, "whether those trees are not in reality one, a Tree of Life for those who do not eat of its fruits and a Tree of Life-and-Death for those who do." It is a question to be pondered on.

In the Avestan tradition, the ancient writings of the Parsees, usually attributed to Zoroaster, there is also mention of two trees, the Tree of the Solar Eagle, which sprang up from the midst of the ocean on the first day, and the Tree of All Seeds, which grew beside it, of which "the seeds, sent down with the rain, are the germs of all living things."

In every country where the tradition is localized the World Tree is held to be of a species indigenous to that country—for Dante it is an apple, in Siberia a birch, and in Scandinavia an oak tree. For Buddhists it is the Bo tree under which the Buddha was sitting when he received his enlightenment. And in fairy tale, which is, one might say, the myth in little, the myth adapted to the fireside, we have the world tree, nothing less, in the story of Jack and the Beanstalk.

There is no tradition in which the tree in some form or other cannot be found. Think of the design of the Kabbalah, the book par excellence of Jewish mysticism, where the symbolical tree of the Sephiroth is shown as a diagram—even, one might say, the backbone—of the cosmos. Indeed, the tree is clearly to be found in the physical makeup of man himself: the great supporting branch of the spinal column, the trellis of bones, where, according to both Hindu and Chinese tradition, the vital forces move up and down like the ascending and descending angels in that other paradigm of the tree that we know as Jacob's ladder.

But there is another powerful aspect of this all-pervading symbol— one less generally known but ranging through many myths and legends—and that is the inverted tree. There are hints of it in Finland and also in Scandinavia, and there is, as well, an Icelandic riddle that asks, "Hast heard where the tree grows of which the crown is on earth and the roots arise in the Heavens?" An Islamic slab in the Byzantine museum at Athens is said to represent an inverted tree supported by two lions. But it is in the earliest writings of Hinduism that one finds it most vividly portrayed, the mysterious

Asvattha Tree of the Rig Veda, with its roots in Heaven and its branches spreading downward. Clearly, this tree has a solar aspect, not so much of a physical as of a supernal sun whose rays strike downward, bringing life. Thinking of this most profound of symbols, one remembers Plato's description of man: "Man," he says, "is a heavenly plant; and what this means is that man is like an inverted tree, of which the roots tend Heavenward and the branches downward to earth." And as one symbol invariably leads to another, this in turn reminds us of the Hanged Man of the Tarot cards, who is shown hanging by one foot from the bough of a tree as he swings head downward through the air, his face turned earthward, serene and joyous. And all these can be assimilated to Gurdjieff's system, whose great symbol, the Ray of Creation, is also an inverted tree, rooted above in the Absolute and descending as an octave through ever denser stages of being from one *Do* to another. Clearly the message of this many-faceted symbol is that the roots of man are not on earth but in Heaven and his meaning is that of the Prodigal Son, who, once he arrives at the lowest level, must, if he is to save his life, arise and go to his Father.

Thus do the symbols endlessly repeat themselves, or perhaps it would be truer to say that the one and self-same symbol gives off a light in every direction, just as myths appear in different guises in many times and places. But I think we have to remember that though myth and symbol are an integral part of the traditions, bound up with them, inextricably woven with them, the traditions are not merely myth and symbol. They exist in their own right. They have resisted and continue to resist all our modern attempts to relieve ourselves of responsibility by turning them into fiction. They are so constituted, so replete with meaning that, do what we will—deny, depreciate, or ignore them—we cannot thrust them out of existence. Nor do they need to be restated, no matter how we ourselves may change. They are part of that wisdom which is, as Saint Augustine put it, "Wisdom uncreate, the same now as it ever was and ever will be." And their purpose remains what it has always been—to relate the unknowable to the known and to speak in all their varying tongues the unnamable name from the burning bush. They are here to declare to us the truth, never put better than in the words of the old Greek poet Aratus, in a phrase that seems to me to sum up all the lectures in this series. He said "Full of Zeus are the cities, full of Zeus are the harbors, full of Zeus are all the ways of men."

QUESTIONS AND ANSWERS

Q: *Is there any special way to present a myth to a child, or should one simply just read it to him and let him get out of it what he will?*

TRAVERS: I'm all for a child taking what he can. Just today I was told the story of someone who had been reading aloud out of a book called All and Everything with her child playing nearby. Soon this child, who is under five, was heard quoting from this book, which is a very grown-up, allegorical work. Children like to be given things that reach higher than their capacities; they like to have to reach for things. I was brought up on Kingsley's stories of the heroes, and I've never forgotten them and have given them to children ever since. But the most important thing is that you should first know the myths yourself. You need to read the story and get to know the story and wait with it and stay with it so that it will drop its meaning into you.

Q: *Would you say something about the prevalence of the three brothers in so many myths?*

TRAVERS: That's a wonderful theme. It always happens that the first brother sets out, handsome and proud, on the quest given to him by his father to find the smallest dog or the most wonderful princess in the world. And he feels that he's perfectly able to find it. So he stops at the crossroads and gets hung up there with all the pleasures of the tavern and so on. He fails in his quest. So the second brother sets forth, and perhaps the second brother has different qualities. Thinking how clever he is, he too gets caught in the tavern. Then the third brother sets out. Now on the way, the brothers nearly always meet a helpful friend—a little old man, or a frog—something by the wayside that offers to help them. But the first two brothers are too strong and clever to accept help. So they continue on. But the youngest brother is always a simpleton, isn't he, and when he meets the frog or the little old man he sits down beside him and says, "Yes, tell me, I'd be only too glad of it because I really don't know." And in the end, of course, it's always the youngest brother, the simpleton, who wins the princess. It always happens so, doesn't it?

But we have to ponder in ourselves who the frog is, or who the little old man is, and who, indeed, the brothers are. I used to think that the three brothers were just three brothers, three single men.

But now I've come to think of them as a composite man, of man on his life's journey. Man who sets forth first believing that he can do anything because of his handsomeness, youth, and wonderful energy. And he finds he can't. So next he thinks, if I'm clever I can bring it off, I can do it, I can find the princess. But he too fails. And in his third stage, if he's fortunate, he comes to realize that he doesn't know anything. And he takes help from what he finds by the roadside. It seems to me that the story of the three brothers is a chart of man's journey through life.

Q: You said that if all the myths were cut off, children would re-create them. How do you account for that? Do you feel that it comes from the racial unconscious or from outside sources?

TRAVERS: I don't think a myth can come to children from outside sources. I think it comes from their point of view of truth, the truth of truth, not the truth of fact. It grows in them, as it were, from their own inward life. One little boy once said to me, "Would you tell me a story?" and I said, "No, I'm tired of telling you stories; you tell me a story for a change." So this three-year-old child said, "Once upon a time I were walking along and I came to a house and inside the house were three wise old woman-ladies. And I knocked on the door and they said, 'Who's there?' and I said 'John.' So they bite-ed me and I spanked them." Well, I've recounted that story many times, but do you see what he was finding? He was finding the Three Fates. The Three Fates bite us all—pretty badly, sometimes. But he had strength to face his life because he spanked the Fates. I thought it was a good omen for him, for his growing up.

Q: What are the Three Fates?

TRAVERS: The weaver, the spinner, and the one that cuts off the thread of man's life. Now that's an excuse for you to look up Greek mythology. But don't let it be long before you discover them, because it's well worth while relating your life to them. And if you could spank the Three Fates, it would be very fortunate.

.

Two Vedantas:
The Best and
the Worst of India

Philippe Lavastine

. . .
.

VEDANTA IS commonly thought to be the basic cultural force of India. But this is true only because India has not yet learned to discriminate between the spurious and the genuine, the best and the worst in the huge mass of Vedantic teachings.

Living in India for many years, I learned from a pupil of the great Pandit Madhusudana of Jaipur that two Vedantas must be discerned: the good Vedanta of the ancients, which really was the *anta* or end, meaning fulfillment, accomplishment, of the Vedic way of life; and the bad Vedanta, which can only be called by the same name if we remember that the word *anta*, end, may also mean destruction, annihilation. There is a recent brand of Vedanta that ignores everything in the Veda (which it despises), a Vedanta that sees and teaches only the top of the mountain, *despising and obscuring its slopes and the paths which can actually take us there.*

The first Vedanta was life-giving, and its tradition, where it still exists, continues to give to India its incomparable light and its most delicate fragrance. It is for such Vedanta that so many people in the world love India, Mother India.

But what of the other side of India? What of the misery that is also one of its features? For while you may proclaim the glory of Indian spirituality, how can you explain this dark side? It is no use saying that invaders and colonizers brought this ruin. It is true. But why did it happen so easily without the slightest resistance worthy of the name? We have to admit that something went wrong with the Hindu spirituality, the Hindu Vedanta.

Pandit Madhusudana Ojha pointed unwaveringly to one single factor: the distinction between a Vedanta that works for the good of the whole collectivity and a so-called "Vedanta" that crept in later and that cared only for the deliverance of the individual. This "Vedanta" (in quotation marks) was inevitably death-giving, for the private good and the public good do not always entail each other. While the public good necessarily brings in its wake the good of the individual, the reverse does not irrevocably follow. For if you say, "Why should I care primarily for the kingdom and its justice?" you must necessarily destroy both the kingdom and the people living in it.

And that is the worst side of India, this "Vedanta" that is always claiming the unreality of the world, saying that it is sheer *Maya*, illusion. But Maya, from the Vedic standpoint, was never understood as illusion. It meant symbol, *pratika* or *vigraha* in Sanskrit. Symbol: that means similitude, reflection. But to take all things as symbols is precisely to redeem the world which we murder when we remain attached to its objects, never understanding that these things of the world are also signs, *deva*, rather than only *bhutas* (material entities).

This is the first key that will help us to distinguish between the best and the worst Vedanta. The first Vedanta never saw in this world anything but symbols, but the last Vedanta never even uses the word. This bad Vedanta repeats *ad nauseam* that we must turn our backs on the objects of the senses. From the very beginning, it claims that the things of the world are *vishayas*, things endued with poison (*visha*), never remembering that the Lord Shiva is named Nila Kantha, meaning "blue throat," an allusion to the high feat of drinking the blue poison called Hala Hala, which first appeared during the churning of the Ocean of Milk at the creation of the world.

And now this Shiva, the Great Lord, for this reason is equated with the peacock because of its blue throat and the splendor of its *mandala*, the circle of its unfurled tail. The wheel is even in our day the emblem of India, inscribed on its flag. But more important than this wheel, the Dharmacakra, which the Lord Buddha set in motion, is the perfect circle of the peacock's tail, because it is adorned with a multiplicity of lesser circles, called eyes, meaning that the One Divine never crushes others down, but adorns Himself with innumerable replicas of his own Infinity, whose perfect symbol is the circle.

Is God, the Supreme Principle, one or multiple? To this question, the Vedas answer: In Himself He is One, but He is multiple in His children.

Participation, the key word of ancient Vedanta, was ascribed first of all to the Deity. By participation we mean, with Durkheim, the power of being at the same time oneself and others. The ancient Vedas stressed this unique feature of the Highest Principle by forbidding the name monism and by speaking of it as simply nondual, Two-in-One, a union more one than unity itself.

Let us understand that though the words may remain the same (*Advaita, Atman, Brahman*), the meaning may drain away leaving a dead shell, a verbalism, a metaphysical stunt.

It happened in India—as it happened in the West—that the Peacock Throne of God, the King of Kings, the One and Only Great King, was completely forgotten. Since so many usurpers had occupied the Peacock Throne, generation after generation, the belief arose that the truth of the divine city could never be revived. As a result, everything social was rejected as worldly, inferior, and, in the last analysis, illusory—Maya.

In this way the new Vedanta appeared. God exists for the individual alone; he has nothing to do with social order and collective life. Religion is a private affair—in the words of Whitehead, "God is what a man does with his own solitude."

We die from this nonsense! If the best Vedanta does not remember itself . . . then what will be the future of man on this planet?

I say the "best Vedanta," but as you will see from what follows, I mean by that the best, the truest, and the most real understanding of the force of tradition in the life of mankind. It is not only India's question; it is a question asked by earth to heaven.

CREATION

The creation myth of the *Rig Veda* is entitled the Hymn of Man and it speaks to us about the *dismemberment of man*. It is the foundation myth of the Hindu culture (*Sams Kriti*), their story of a God All, called Man (*Purusha*), who was dismembered by the gods, his own senses, at the beginning, and has now to be re-membered.

A fall. With powerful images the Vedic seer tells us that "the skull of man (became) the sky, his eyes the sun and the moon, his breath the wind, his navel the atmosphere . . . his feet the earth." And a resurrection, when the creature, his *membra disjecta*, came back to recollect Him, at the call of the *Brahmana*.

It is in *Rig Veda* X, 90, 72 that we find the first mention of the four castes: *Brahmana, Kshatriya* (those whose function is protection,

Kshatra), *Vaishya* (the people), and *Shudra,* the servants.

Here is the extraordinary passage:

> His mouth was of a Brahmana
> The Kshatriyas came back to reconstitute His arms,
> The Vaishyas came back to reconstitute His thighs,
> The Shudras issued from His feet (as His shadow).

The formulations may appear to be very different in the creation myths of the other traditions. Nevertheless there is a point which is always the same—namely, that there was before the creation a Wholeness or Holiness that was dispersed at the *beginning,* giving place to everything we may perceive. We must emphasize that the fall and resurrection of Man is described as the fall and resurrection of a *collective man.*

In the same way, Adam in the Bible is a collective personality.

Now—a distinction between fall and sacrifice. The first creation, SRSTI, happens as the result of a fall—of a forgetting of oneself. The second creation (KRTI—"well-created," or *Sams Kriti*) happens as the result of a sacrifice, as a conscious action. In SRSTI everything proceeds by itself, mechanically—spreading outward and downward indefinitely, as it is told in the Kabbalah, where God, seeing this mechanical, indefinite out-spreading of the first creation, shouts out, *"Enough!"*

Since it is mechanical, it spreads outward without control. God must establish limits. A *horizon.*

Limit in this sense contains, brings us back to ourselves, to a remembering. In Indian myth this limitation is known as the "great arms of the Black" (the darkness of Krishna).

Like the blackness that surrounds and limits all light and energy, there is a cosmic need for real limit which brings reality to itself. No light can go farther than a definite horizon. The idea of a divine horizon can be understood if we remember that the sublime is what remains within its limit—*sub-limen.*

LEGEND

Why have we lost the legends?—and are we not in danger of dying from cold because of this loss? We forget that a legend is a tale that has to be understood with intelligence. But for this intelligence to bear fruit, it must lead to action. Legend must be lived.

Legenda are tales that have to be understood, but if you do not act accordingly, you will never acquire the ambrosia, the nectar of imperishable being. Your understanding cannot remain in your head. When you *act* in accordance with legend, only then do you understand with your head, your arms, your feet, your belly, your whole presence. This is what we have forgotten about the understanding of legends—and, indeed, about all understanding.

Let us take, for example, the legend of the hero and the dragon— a central legend of India as well as of all other cultures. It was not meant as an entertainment but as a guide to life. Think of the dragon as the collective, the collective personality of the *patriarchal reality*. We speak of a collectivity with a head, a real *head*, a chief in the root meaning of the word. This needs to be emphasized.

To the individual, the patriarchal reality appears dragonlike (draconian).

But we must not speak yet of the individual. We speak of the *dividual*. "Individual" means, literally, not divisible. But we are divisible, you and I. We are divided within ourselves, we are a multiplicity, in conflict and suffering. We are not only dividuals, we are poor, poor dividuals.

In this legend of the dragon, the hero is the dividual who refuses to be eaten by the corporate personality, the patriarchal reality.

Yet, for the dividual, if he is eaten, he is saved—he becomes the dragon. We need to be eaten by this dragon.

In the *Shatapatha Brahmana* we have the story of the Purusha Prajapati rushing toward the creatures, with his mouth wide open, so much so that they are terrified. But he tells them, "Don't be afraid! If I eat you, each of you will find his true place in my Body!"

THE TWO VEDANTAS

We speak of two Vedantas, and we may equally speak of two Indias. There is the India of the Brahmins and the India of the yogis. It is incomprehensible that they live together. Yet they do live together, and the life of India is made up of these two lives. It was the same in ancient China, where there existed a state religion of Confucianism and the individualistic religion of Taoism.

The yogi is fundamentally anarchical, individualistic. He cares only for ecstasy, for personal liberation, freedom from every collective discipline. He takes upon himself many disciplines, but only for himself. I have seen many such men. A yogi who holds up his arms for months and years without moving them until they become frozen, stiff as wood. A remarkable achievement, but he has to be fed by others. This is a symbol of a way of living, of the man who wants his own truth, a wonder of a man who is yet for himself only. Such a man does everything for his divine self, his godliness.

Such is the yogi. The Brahmin does not even look at the yogi. He lives in a larger reality, one well ordered, well limited, well horizoned, as we might say. In most parts of India the name of a Brahmin ends with this dignifying word: *Sharma*—meaning *serene*. The *Nirukta*, which is India's treatise about the art of charging words with meaning, explains *sharma* by quite another word, *carma*, meaning *skin*. And the book explains that the only way of keeping serenity is never to transgress one's own skin. The Brahmins say, "We tie our petty selves with collective rituals in order to find liberation."

We may say of these Brahmins that they are notaries for the supernatural. A notary is not a very amusing person. Yet these notaries in their way have been the great artists who have shaped the civilization of India. The word "Brahmin" means shaper, former— like an unseen stage director who forms the reality before us. They directed the consecration of Kings, unlike our Christian priests always fighting for supremacy over "Caesar." The so-called "Laws of Manu" contain an important word on this: "The Brahmin of this land does not teach others his own law, but theirs."

The yogi, on the other hand, teaches his own law. He says to everyone, "Look what a master I am!"

The civilization of the ancient Hebrews was also made by these notaries for the supernatural.

Two Vedantas, then: the Vedanta of the Brahmins and the Vedanta of the yogis. The first proceeding by steps, *krama mukti*, the second believing in the possibility of an immediate, explosive, orgasmic illumination. For the Brahmin there is no romanticism at all in this *samadhi*. Such *samadhi* appears when the mind is in the right place, well concentrated, as it is said.

There is a story of the great Mullah Nasr Eddin, the legendary wise simpleton of the Islamicized East. It happened one day that the Mullah had to play his part as a *cadi*, a judge. Two plaintiffs appear, each of them saying that the other is a devil and that he is a pure angel. Mullah hears them with the greatest attention and says to each of them, "You are right." An onlooker is astonished and says to Mullah, "But they contradict each other on every point. How can they both be right?" And Mullah answers, "You are right!"

Our Brahmins and yogis contradict each other in the same way. What is the key? We have to understand that the yogi is not wrong because he believes in grace, but because his *askesis* (asceticism) is a systematic forcing of grace. When the Doctor of the Law, the humble Brahmin, is taken by a rapture into a Seventh Heaven, like Saint Paul, it is felt as a catastrophic invasion of the divine in a well-formed, sacred world that is utterly transcended from within and not broken from without as is the case with the yogi.

Such stories as those of Mullah Nasr Eddin are a means of transmitting ideas. Mullah is right when he says that both the yogi and the Brahmin are right because both are only aspects of a living, suffering collective body that necessarily envelops the two standpoints of the yogi and the Brahmin.

We may say that it was a catastrophe for India when Shankaracarya in the eighth century translated the Upanishads into conceptual, philosophical language. He thought that by this he would open the teachings. But it was not an opening; it was a shutting. It was Coomaraswamy who said that to have lost the art of thinking in images is to have fallen into the verbalism of philosophy.

If the present need is new thought, new thinking, let us attend to such stories more respectfully. It is such new thought—which is really ancient thought—that the story hints at. There is a higher logic of complementarity, a logic of mediation through social feeling. Social feeling is *love*.

Revolutionary thought and cyclical reality. Our thought and our action must become *cosmomimetic*, a reflection of the universal law. What other meaning is there to the phrase "being in contact with reality"?

Is it night or day? Does the turning wheel go upward or downward? According to our linear logic these two movements—ascending and descending—contradict each other. Either you are progressing or regressing, and there is no third alternative. But Eastern thought knows about a *Bhavacakra*, the wheel of Existence. And when one part of the circumference of the wheel is going downward it means that the opposite—not contradictory—part is going upward. In other words, there is no progression of one part of the whole without the corresponding regression of another part. And if we care, as we should, only for the whole, we have to understand that even if such progress is not possible without a progress of the parts, the excessive progress of one part may be a definite obstacle to the progress of the whole. Hence this part will have to be sacrificed by the King—I mean, the Spirit responsible for the common good.

SRSTI OR INFRACREATION

The literal meaning is ejaculation. Millions of spermatozoa are thrown out, but only one will fertilize the ovum—*if it is received*. All others must perish because the Infinite Possibility can never *manifest* entirely. Such are the conditions of the ovum.

The maternal side stands on the side of Grace. And now let us well understand that the Brahmins of India stand on the side of Rigor, as it has been said, "Let us first create a Mother, out of whom we might be reborn."

This mother is a social community, called *ecclesia* in the West and *sangha* in India. Inside a *sangha*, not every possibility is allowed to manifest. But if a possibility, a grace from the divine Father, is received, the spiritual seed that has been elected will be born into a real child. *It will not remain a possibility; there will be an effective realization.*

That is why it is said in India that the SRSTI of the Father is not enough. There must be ATISRSTI—*ati* means beyond—which means *a second creation*.

This second creation is called KRTI or Samskriti. This is creation in its proper meaning, according to the root *kr*, which we find in the words *karman*—literally, action of creating in order; or *samskaras* —usually translated as "sacraments," but meaning literally actions in order to create a being *completely*, actions necessary in order to create a complete being (SAM).

The yogis stand on the level of the SRSTI. The Brahmins alone know of the SAMSKRTI or the art of making a thing complete. And the thing about which they care first of all is the *state*. How often I have heard it said in India, "Never say Church and State!" What is the state? It is the normal church, the normal city, temple, led by those who follow the norm (*dharma*)—that is, the final goal of the life of man.

A state that does not know the norm is no state at all. Western "states," being completely ignorant of the norm, are "e-normous" monsters. And why? It is because the Brahmins of the West never cared for the birth of a true *Dharmarajah*, King of Justice, Melchizedek, King of Salem (peace). Yet the Brahmins of the West still speak of *Mater Ecclesia*, but they have forgotten the whole point: the Birth, the *Incarnation* of their Christ in a real King. Without a center, there can be no *mandala* (circus, *Kirche*).

The concentration of the Divine in a point, the Throne (Greek: *thronos* = Sanskrit: *dharman*—literally, action of sustaining) is the whole work of the Brahmins, who do not simply support the Throne, as is commonly said. *They are the Throne, and may be called the Isis of India.* Their Son is the King, Horus, the Face of God turned toward the world. They are themselves the invisible side of the Deity, its very secret, and that is why they have to remain unmanifest. The glory is for the King and not for us who are his mother.

And do you know why things went the way they did in the West? Look here—this is a rising sun: . How do you read it? A Westerner will see it as the symbol of a victory of Light over Darkness. But for us Brahmins, who must always stay in *the superluminous Night of the divine*, it must be read as the Victory of the Cow of Night giving birth to the Golden Calf, the *Bambino, oriens*, as the Divine Kid is called in the church liturgy of Christmas. Only the King, who is endowed with spiritual power by the Brahmins, can bring the reign of God, the *Ramraj* upon earth, and by the instrumentality of its *divine power* (never say "temporal power!") the Peace of God that "passeth understanding." The same is said in our Vedas about the Great King of Heaven, Varuna: "His Power gives wisdom to all the creatures." But in the West, you see, all this is topsy-turvy.

And that is why you care so much for all our feeble yogis, and not for us Brahmins who could be creators of powerful Kings. Nowadays, things have gone so far that people call a miserable yogi sitting in the street adorned only with the ornament of his lice a *Maharaj*! This yogi, however, is still in the SRSTI, in a complete confusion of mind concerning the science of the possible and the impossible. He has not even a faint idea of what we call culture, *Samskriti*, in our Sanskrit language, which he blissfully ignores and even despises.

Beneath the world of names and forms of our notaries there is the "world" of ignominy and deformity, the *inframormal*. Although the world of form stands below the "world" of the superformal or the universal, we must understand that in relation to the first "creation" of the *Asuras*, SRSTI, whose symbol is the dark forest (*aranya*), the chaos of infinite possibility, the second creation is that of the clearing (*loka*) which is obtained by burning down, by sacrificing a part of the dark forest in order to obtain a *place* (locus, lodge) *from within which we might be born to an orderly life.*

The Profane, the Sacred (the fanum), *and the Divine.* We are always leaping from one extreme to another, forgetting the middle world, the mesocosmos of the Sacred. For instance, Christians still quarrel about the meaning of the expression, "Give us this day our daily bread." For "materialist" Christians, it is the "real" bread that is meant, while for "spiritualist" Christians it has always been understood as the bread of the angels, *fanum supersubstantialum, ton arton epiousioun.* But the true interpretation is that a sacred precept has not only to be learned by heart *each day*—it was also called the *manducation* (the eating) of the lesson, the lesson put into practice, according to the words of Jesus, "My food is to do the will of my Father."

The world of the Sacred alone deserves to be called the world of a MANAVA, meaning real man in Sanskrit, real because having MANU (ATMAN in its legislative aspect) as his center. Beyond the world of men live the gods; and below, the animals. And we must realize how wrong Durkheim was when he confused the Sacred with the Divine on one side and with the social on the other side. He wished to oppose these three to the "world" of the uninitiated individuals, equated by him, justly, with the profane. Durkheim's idea of the Divine, being nothing more than a mystical hypostasis of the social, was complete nonsense, which veiled the truth of its equation of the social with the Sacred.

In this equation, however veiled it was, Durkheim was nevertheless more profound than Rudolf Otto or Mircea Eliade, who have also equated the Sacred with the Divine, missing—in an opposite way— the real nature of the Sacred. Once they relegate the social to the realm of the profane, they have unwittingly adopted the yogi's view of things.

But God can descend only in the realm of the Sacred, the sacramental, or well-formed social order (*Shakyamuni*: Shakya-soci-branches; *muni*-the trunk, the *axis mundi*; therefore, *Shakyamuni*: the tree of life, savior, and king). God appears in the middle realms, the realm of the Brahmin.

Let us take it as our task to discriminate between the real or sacred collective man, and the infrahuman collectivity of totalitarian states in all their modes, subtle and obvious. The sacred collectivity is superhuman, supraindividual in that it brings the saving force to the mutilated dividuals that we are.

Two Vedantas. The Fall always takes place at the end (*anta*) of a Veda (vision). That is why we can never rest only on personal vision. We need collective ritual life. We need to be supported by a sacred year "in heaven" and a sacred geography "on earth." "Thy Kingdom come, thy will be done, on earth as it is in heaven." We repeat the words like parrots and every trace of a mythical or sacred geography has disappeared from our so-called civilized countries.

But the Fall is a necessity—because it brings suffering in its wake. And when we suffer, we remember. When things again begin to "go quite well"—that is, in a completely mechanical way—we forget Him again. And there is a new fall, a new war, new miseries for a new Remembering.

> In suffering all men Remember,
> In happiness no one who can.
> If in happiness man could Remember,
> What need for suffering then?

Therefore, the question arises: How could it be possible to remember Him even when we are not distressed? The answer is: our whole life needs to be ritualized, that is, submitted to voluntary sufferings for the individual in order to realize the state of nonsuffering for the city, the corporate whole. In the salvation of the city, you will find your deliverance, *moksha*. But the contrary is not true at all. More than that: the so-called deliverance of an individual alone cannot but disequilibrate the life of the whole city, *if it is not a deliverance that takes place in the center, on the throne.* If one man is a saint, he has to be the King.

But who shall decide the sanctity of a man? The disciples are always shouting out that their own master is the greatest saint, the greatest maharishi, the greatest maharaj. . . .

The word "Vedanta" is late. In Vedic times, they said, *Anansa Vedah!*: "The Vedas are without end, infinite!" Later, the word Vedanta (*Veda + anta*) was taken to mean fulfillment, consummate, complete achievement (ANSA) of the vision of the Divine in the fourth stage of life of the *sannyasi,* the man of *complete* renunciation.

Vedic seers did not call themselves Vedantins, because they were still active. But we find now everywhere in India men who are still living in one of the inferior stages of life, called the stage of the student (*brahma-charya*), the stage of the householder (*grmastha*), or the stage of the "Senator" (*vana-prasth*), the man who has forsaken all concern for his own family so as to devote himself to the public good. But now Vedanta has become a private philosophic *opinion*, precisely that which was called in the West *Airesis* and in Buddhist scriptures *Ditti*, and was forbidden as such. Who are you to decide about the ultimate truth? Is it Advaita, Visishtadvaita, Dvaita, or some mixture of these three systems as in the Vedanta of Vallabha and Nimbuka?

There is this Sanskrit saying: "In a dubious question, you must first ask the *Sruti* (the Vedic revelation); if it brings no answer, ask the *Smrti* (the sacred tradition); if it brings no answer, ask the *Puranas* (the ancient writings); if they bring no answer, ask your family guru; and if he does not see the answer, ask your parents; and if they do not see either, ask your friends—because it is only when every help from outside has failed that one man is allowed to ask his own consciousness to decide about the truth."

Such was the traditional standpoint. How far we are from it. But even further from it is this so-called Vedantin of the streets who really is only divinizing his own opinion.

ATMAN-BRAHMAN

These words have remained for three thousand years, but their meaning has changed. Gradually, progressively, without any violence, a deviation creeps in and the tradition that was life-giving in the beginning ends by becoming death-giving. It always happens in that way.

Then revolutions come inevitably. The sacred tradition of old is accused and discarded abruptly and brutally. But it may happen that the so-called revolutionaries actually bring back the earliest tradition that had slowly been forgotten.

Speaking about "tradition," we must never forget that the word is cognate with "trade" in English and *tradittore* (traitor) in Italian.

The first Christians who did not hide the Gospels from the pagans were called *tradittores*. Similarly, we find at the end of every Upanishad—as in the last chapter of the Bhagavad Gita—terrible warnings against such "*tradittores*." Nevertheless, it happened that the Upanishads finally fell into the hands of each and every person in India, as the Gospels have fallen into our hands in our own times.

The first "Christian" teaching was absolutely "Vedantic," since it taught the Supreme Identity of the Son and the Father, Man and God, Atman and Brahman. But it was never said that this Son was the *dividual* man. He was Man as a whole, as the Assyro-Babylonian tradition has put it so clearly:

> The Shadow of God is Man
>> and men are the Shadow of Man.
> Man is the King,
>> who is the image of God.

In the Epistles of Paul, the Son is depicted as "the very image and imprint of the Father." But a time came when each and every *dividual* attributed to himself the *imago Dei* which pertains only to the *individuum quod non est pars* of the medieval tradition—namely, the Sacred King, called the *Christus Domini*.

Therefore we must rid ourselves of two fateful errors: first, the error committed by "the bad Vedanta," which is to believe that there is a supreme identity between a dividual and the Brahman. Second, the error committed by the Christians when they misunderstood completely the idea of *incarnation*, angrily discarding the perspective of the Jews who wanted the Messiah to be a real King.

There is no doubt that in the High Middle Ages, in Byzantium as well as in the West, the so-called "Constantinian Christianity" was still *traditional*, and that the fall into our "modern times" occurred only in the time of the so-called Re-formation, whose founders had lost every memory of the Form.

Coomaraswamy has clearly shown that the discarding of the idea of transsubstantiation (which is the main point of Christianity) was done for the same reason as the rejection of the idea of the Divinity of the King. The *imbroglio* was hopeless and the so-called "religious wars" of those times had to be atrocious because the Re-formers indeed were nearer the truth concerning Kingship and the "mystery of the Kingdom" than were the friends of the Pope. It was Catholicism that was the main destroyer of the *corpus politicum vel mysticum* of Christ, of the *Purusha*, whose resurrection can never take place in a Church alone, but only in a *Church-State*.

Both Emperors and Popes indeed were right, in a sense, when they wanted to be at the same time Popes and Emperors. The only trouble was that at such times the very idea of a Brahmana had completely disappeared from the West. The Maharaja of India who wore, as it were, the *triregnum* (the symbol of his Power over the three worlds) always prostrated himself at the feet of the naked *sannyasi* when he visited him in secret, asking for spiritual help. But neither the Pope nor the Emperor would have done that. "I Caesar, I Imperator," shouted Pope Boniface VIII. Such a fall of the "spiritual authority" was bound to produce a spiritual revolt. And Christianity disintegrated.

Now we may return to the first meaning of the word *Atman* in Vedic times. To be sure, such a word is an *anugama*, a word whose meaning exists *according to* its context. *Atman is that with which I identify. Tadatmyan*—literally, *That-I*—is the word that means "identification" in Sanskrit. And *that* (*tat*) does not necessarily mean the Supreme *Brahman*. It may mean—and such was the case in the times when the *Brihad Aranyaka Upanishad* was written—my wife, myself, my children, and the goods of my eyes and my ears (the material things I see and the spiritual things I hear).

The *atman* in Vedic times was first of all the social unit, of which I was a *part*. Feeling himself to be a part of the social body greater than his own body, the life of the Vedic man was a *participation* in a life greater than his own. And that very life was *his atman*.

Participation is the key word. We need life, I mean a participation in a greater life than our own. But here lies danger. We may desire that life for ourselves, not for others. We may refuse to play our part in the collective life, believing that *we* are more than a part.

We have already mentioned Durkheim's definition of *participation*: "power to be at the same time one's own self and others." Later, Levy-Brühl maintained that participation was the supreme confusion of the mind, because A is A and, if A is A, how can it be B? And therewith he initiated the concept of a "primitive mind" of old that was, as he said, "completely prelogical." But if a man tells you that he *is* not only himself, but also his wife and his children, will you shout that such a man is prelogical?

The point is—and it cannot be stressed too much—that we *need* the Absolute. Relativity is meaningless and boring. *Homo capax Dei.* And if this *need* is not taken into consideration, the result for man will inevitably be "existential neurosis," the endless, empty, gnawing groping for "the meaning of life."

But I ask you to pay attention. There is a terrible pitfall—that pretention that may appear when a poor dividual lays claim to having found Absolute Truth. It is complete nonsense! Yet there is a desire at the root of this whole pretention that is perfectly real and authentic, a tremendous desire to escape endless relativity, a desire to *participate* in something *real, divine,* or *absolute.* And this desire may be and must be satisfied.

It is the *present need.*

And *sacred tradition,* if rightly understood, may show us the ways of satisfying it.

Atman indeed was the *Brahman* in ancient Aryan India, but not at all in the way our modern Vedantins take it—because the *Brahman* was then understood rightly as the totality of the "sacred formulas" (*brahman*), rituals, and sacraments (*samskaras*) by which the family, on a lesser scale, and the Kingdom, on the greater scale, could be maintained in a good state of mind and in good health as a corporate whole, where the dividuals could find their Individuality in a greater Person than their petty selves.

The Upanishads say it quite clearly: "Everything which is not the *Atman* is misery." But traitorous-*tradittore*-tradition came, for whom the experience of a participative life in a greater whole had become *res ignota,* a thing unknown.

And as it is said, *ignoti nulla cupido* (that which is unknown cannot be desired). Therefore they translated their word *Atman* by the words "Ultimate Reality."

But the *Atman-Brahman* of a family, of a kingdom, even if it is greater than my own *atman,* nevertheless falls very far short of an *ultimate reality.* To be sure, it is still a mortal *atman*—but *precisely as such it may be offered, when it has become perfected* (*samskrita*) —*that is, worthy of being offered,* in the fire of sacrifice to the Absolute. And such sacrifice, the sacrifice of the *collective man, the regenerated Adam,* whose prototype among us was Christ, may be the means for the descent of the Divine in Man—not man in the singular to the exclusion of others.

Just as *psyche* and *theos* are not to be confused with psychology and theology, which are the science of the soul and the science of God, so myth must not be equated with mythology, the interpretation of myths, the attempt to trap their meaning.

For each myth—for example, the Christian myth—how many mythologies do we have! And all claim to be the sole and only interpretation. In this they are all of them wrong because each myth admits of many interpretations. And the deeper interpretations will not necessarily be the best for men who still stand at a very superficial level of understanding.

And that is why it may be good sometimes simply to recite, to re-ex-cite, the ancient myths without caring for their symbolism. The myth has first to be taken *as you like it*, as you find your way into it. Only keep it in your memory and, some day, you may suddenly shout: "It is *that* which the myth wanted to tell me *and I did not understand it!*"

Myths are time-bombs.

Here are two of them.

I. A STORY OF ARJUNA

This tale takes place before the *Mahabharata* war. Arjuna, at last, has understood that he cannot remain hiding in a corner, but that he has to manifest, to fight—that is, to win or die. But he had nothing in his hands but a human sword, his own resolution. He realized that he needed a divine sword and decided to visit Shiva, in his Himalayan abode. Great were the obstacles, the demons, the doors he had to open with his sword along the way. Success followed success. But as he was nearing the top of the mountain, a huge dragon blocked his way. The path was narrow and Arjuna had to choose whether to flee or fight. Arjuna sensed that he would die in this struggle and he begged the monster to give him respite so that he could offer a last sacrifice to Shiva. The dragon agreed. And with some small stones Arjuna erected an altar to Shiva. He gathered red flowers along the side of the path and wove them into a garland which he placed atop the altar.

He knelt down to worship the Lord, dying in his prayer. And when, regenerated, he turned again for battle, he felt such power in his arms that he had no doubt he would cut off the head of the beast with one stroke. But at that moment he saw the very garland of flowers which he had set upon the altar resting now upon the head of the dragon.

II. A STORY OF THE RAMAYANA

Once upon a time, at dawn, the great bell was struck that stood at the door of the palace of Rama. A mighty sound. And the King awoke suddenly and sprang from his bed, knowing that the sound of that bell meant someone had been the victim of injustice.

There at the gate stood a Brahmin with his young son dead in his arms. "It is supposed to be Ramraj, the Golden Age," said the father, his voice trembling with sorrow and anger. "Yet here, look! Seven years old and death has taken him!"

For Rama it was enough. He understood at once that some crime had been left unpunished in his Kingdom and that the blot was upon him. He took down his great bow and went out into the land, inquiring near and far. Soon he discovered a Shudra named Shambuka who had forsaken his duties and instead was practicing Yoga at the door of the city. Without a moment's hesitation, Rama released his arrow, killing Shambuka. At that very instant the Brahmin child returned to life as the Shudra attained his goal: the Death divine, liberation, from the very hands of the Lord.

THE KALI YUGA

Throughout India you will hear a beautiful story which is at the same time a prayer. Its refrain is, "Take us to the other shore!" But we are asked to understand that the other shore, like the Kingdom, is always "at hand." God is not a goal to be attained at the end of a long road. The road starts from God. The *Satya Yuga*, the Golden Age, is always waiting for man.

But at some point an invention crept into the tradition. People began to think and to say that the Age of Truth lies in the distant past and that we are condemned to live cut off from that glorious arising of light; we are irrevocably denizens of the *Kali Yuga*.

The ancient view was actually quite different. It said that each of us is in the *Kali Yuga* as long as we have not yet taken the first steps of Yoga. The words *yuga* and *Yoga* are the same. A community that lives according to the teachings with individuals who strive along the path of Yoga—at any moment such a community can enter the *Satya Yuga*.

This is a striking example of how an idea becomes death-giving when taken in an external meaning only.

And what about the *samadhi* (illumination, ecstasy) which is at the end of the yogic path and is, as well, the goal of the Vedantin? The word is understandable only in contrast to *vyadhi*, which means distress—literally: displaced mind, infirm mind. In other words, the mind (*dhi*) fallen from its correct place at the center of Man. Man in Sanskrit is called *purusha*, literally: the holy fire which burns in the city (*pura*), or *manava*, literally: son of Manu. And *Manu* means "Center of Man." Now the Center is never far, though we may fall very far from our Center. But the vision of it may take place at any time, *if we are reminded.*

It is said that God is the starting point of the road. But it is not said that there is no road, no work to be done upon ourselves. The point that matters is that the Beginning is on the top of the mountain. In order to say *in principio, en arke, bereshit*, the Sanskrit language says: *Agre*. It means: on the peak of the mountain, where the first sacrifice takes place. Read, for this, "creation of the world" (what we have called the second or real creation).

Therefore, the work to be done is not a work of de-creation but a work of allowing the spiritual influence that is received in the sacrifice to descend over all the slopes of the world mountain. The work must always begin from the summit, which is equally the center of the world-wheel. The mind has to radiate. It has to extend (TAN —thus: *tantra*) all over the world, *but without losing its Center, its state of samadhi.*

The whole difficulty of the work lies here. And that is why so many people in India have lost the ancient doctrine so clearly formulated in these two words: *Samadarshanam; Vishamavartanam*, meaning "equality" (*sama*) in vision; "differentiation" in action.

This was interpreted as meaning that seeing all things as equal (*Sama-darshanam—samadhi*)—meant the disappearance of the world since the world we know is so differentiated. But the primordial idea was completely different. The idea was that what was needed was *detachment* in order that there could be real, objective *participation* in the life the world, without the fall into forgetfulness of our real Self.

All the creatures cried out to the awakened one, the Buddha, "O Compassionate!"

EXPANSION AND CONTRACTION

The story of Rama and Shambuka has shown us that the ancient world knew about *nidanas*, hidden connections. All things hang together. We are living within a Whole. If there is a disturbance at the periphery, the fall of a Shudra from the duties of his caste, it can bring about such disorders as the death of a Brahmin boy. Then, what about a disorder in the Center?

Such a disorder in the Center would inevitably destroy the entire web of our corporate life. Destroyed at its root would be the *vine*, the *atman*, all the branches—called *Shakya* in Sanskrit and *socii* in Latin. If the Truth is not enthroned in the middle of the temple-palace, which is built in the middle of the *capital* (the head—Latin, *caput*) of the whole kingdom—then disorder, war, famine, and death everywhere and for all things.

Hence we understand now the tremendous importance of the divine right of Kings. If they are not divinely ordained, if a usurper has taken over, if he sits in the middle, the tree of life will soon be struck by the thunderbolt of Zeus or Yahweh.

One day I asked a friend, a learned rabbi, "Can you tell me in brief the message of the whole Bible?"

He answered, "I can. The Bible is nothing but God shouting these two words, 'ENTHRONE ME!' "

It was as though a flash of light instantly dispelled from my mind a doubt that had long been lingering over it. And I told him in one breath about the last words of Shankaracarya, which are unfortunately so much admired by modern Vedantins: "O my Lord, forgive me that I went to search for you in your temples, forgetting that you are everywhere."

The rabbi exploded. "Such was the Fall," he said. "That is pantheistic spirituality, the blotting out of any differentiation between the Lord and his creatures. And our own Solomon," he said, "was already beginning to be infected with this plague when he uttered nearly the same words: 'O my Lord, I shall do your will and build your sanctuary, but why do you need a Center, when you are everywhere?' "

Life is rhythm, Great Life is great rhythm, expansion and contraction, the giving out and the taking in, the Wings of Garuda, the bird of Vishnu. But the expansion, the giving out, must be conscious.

All beings breathe, even God.

SACRED TRADITION AND PRESENT NEED

The present need is God. But we have to understand that the true God is the collective consciousness of the City. *God is not the animator of a personal consciousness proceeding by assertion and the exclusion of others.* When such men appear they are not the representatives of God. They are the "great men" of the West—conquerors in the line of damnation which is led by Alexander, Caesar, Napoleon, and Hitler.

Asserting individuals are the exact opposite of the present need. We have to understand together. If we do not understand together, the understanding has no value. And most of the gurus of India proceed by exclusion and assertion—the exclusion of all other points of view. That was not the case in ancient, Vedic, India.

In ancient India there was no orthodoxy. *Orthodoxy is the opposite of the present need.* Orthopraxis and orthopoiea—yes. The "lonely crowd" has to be formed into a social body, awakened to a corporate life. Things have to be done correctly. The art of living together has to be learned and practiced. That is the need. The sacred, the form of the social whole, has to come back into being.

Mohammed said, "My community cannot proffer error."

And the great saying of At-Tabari—who in the modern world understands this saying? "When a scholar studies the Koran and comes to the truth by his own judgment, it is not the truth, because he has come to it by his own judgment." Because the ego has crept in there.

The greatest Vedanta is life-giving, as was expressed by the holiest of Sufis, Ibn Arabi, who said, "The divine essence must invade man as would death, as a power that takes hold of him. Were it not so, the divine essence could be taken from man by death." For us there cannot be anything immortal, if we are not first annihilated by the divine. If then this death takes hold of us, what can ordinary death do? It does not exist.

Notes on the Contributors

Jacob Needleman, professor of philosophy at San Francisco State University, is author of *The New Religions* and *A Sense of the Cosmos*, a study of modern science and the search for consciousness. He is also the General Editor of the Penguin Metaphysical Library.

Father William Johnston, s.j., has lived in Japan for more than twenty years and is the author of *The Still Point, Christian Zen*, and the recently published *Silent Music: The Science of Mysticism*.

Lobsang P. Lhalungpa was born in Lhasa, Tibet, and has passed through the disciplines of the major branches of Tibetan Buddhism under its greatest masters. He is presently director of a Tibetan-studies institute in Vancouver and is engaged in a far-reaching project of translating the sacred texts of Tibetan Buddhism.

Lizelle Reymond has personally entered into the traditions of India as have few Westerners. She is the author of *My Life with a Brahmin Family, To Live Within*, and, most recently, *Shakti*. She returned to the West in 1954 and now writes and teaches in Geneva, Switzerland.

Seyyed Hossein Nasr is Dean of the Faculty of Arts and Letters at Teheran University, Iran. The author of a great many books and essays dealing with the universal ideas at the heart of all traditions, he has recently published in America *The Encounter of Man and Nature, Ideals and Realities of Islam*, and *Sufi Essays*.

Dom Aelred Graham is a Benedictine monk of Ampleforth Abbey, England. Among his numerous books are *Zen Catholicism, Conversations Christian and Buddhist, The End of Religion*, and the recently published *Contemplative Christianity*. Both he and William Johnston, each in his own way, have opened the possibility of a vitalizing exchange between Christianity and Zen Buddhism.

P. L. TRAVERS, although best known as the author of the world-famous *Mary Poppins*, has been a lifelong student of mythology and fairy tales as bearers of psychological and metaphysical teachings. Her latest book, *Friend Monkey*, is based on the Hindu myth of Hanuman.

PHILIPPE LAVASTINE is a well-known French scholar who has lived and traveled extensively throughout Asia. At present he teaches in Paris, where he is completing a study of the concept of the divine king.